Mission

We understand "community literacy" as the domain for literacy work that exists outside of mainstream educational and work institutions. It can be found in programs devoted to adult education, early childhood education, reading initiatives, lifelong learning, workplace literacy, or work with marginalized populations, but it can also be found in more informal, *ad hoc* projects.

For us, literacy is defined as the realm where attention is paid not just to content or to knowledge but to the symbolic means by which it is represented and used. Thus, literacy makes reference not just to letters and to text but to other multimodal and technological representations as well. We publish work that contributes to the field's emerging methodologies and research agendas.

Subscriptions

We are pleased to offer subscriptions to *CLJ*—two issues per year:
    Institutions & libraries $200.00
    Faculty $30.00
    Graduate students & community workers $20.00
Please send a check or money order made out to the University of Arizona Foundation to:
    John Warnock, *Community Literacy Journal*
    445 Modern Languages Bldg., University of Arizona, P.O. Box 210067
    Tucson, AZ 85721
    Info: johnw@u.arizona.edu

Cover Image

As artist, academic, and public rhetor, Adela C. Licona addresses the surface and the depth of our daily lives through visual, textu/r/al, and lived literacies. With the camera in hand, Licona interrogates the coming together and coming apart at the fold—the inside/outside—of the vivid con/textu/r/al forms and functions across the land, bodies, and built environments. She is interested in detail and its connection to a larger context as a means to provoke and participate in new ways of looking and seeing that allow us to imagine new ways of being and relating particularly around our interconnections to one another and to the earth.

This photo, in particular, considers human relationships to im/mobility and the circulation of goods in a consumer society. From her roadside memorials/descanso series, Licona's images instantiate her interests in the production of im/mobilities and of (contested) knowledges in space—who gets written or otherwise in/visibilized into and out of space through material practices, spatialized mis/representations, and historic accounts. She has started to document (research, archive, photograph, and film) public memorials, especially roadside memorials or descansos in their ephemeral spirit as she sees these public~intimate/intimate~public spaces as spaces of recognition, resistance, and devotional reflection. Her interest in material space, spatialized representations, rhetoric, and public scholarship is manifest in her roadside memorials project.

Editorial Advisory Board

Jonathan Alexander	University of California, Irvine
Nancy Guerra Barron	Northern Arizona University
David Barton	Lancaster University, UK
David Blakesley	Clemson University
Melody Bowdon	University of Central Florida
Tara Brabazon	University of Brighton, UK
Danika Brown	University of Texas–Pan American
Ernesto Cardenal	Casa de los Tres Mundos, Managua
Marilyn Cooper	Michigan Technological University
Linda Flower	Carnegie Mellon University
Diana George	Virginia Tech University
Jeff Grabill	Michigan State University
Greg Hart	Tucson Area Literacy Coalition
Shirley Brice Heath	Stanford University
Tobi Jacobi	Colorado State University
Lou Johnson	River Parishes YMCA, New Orleans
Paula Mathieu	Boston College
Regina Mokgokong	Project Literacy, Pretoria, South Africa
Ruth E. Ray	Wayne State University
Georgia Rhoades	Appalachian State University
Mike Rose	University of California, Los Angeles
Tiffany Rousculp	Salt Lake Community College
Cynthia Selfe	The Ohio State University
Tanya Shuy	National Institute for Literacy
Vanderlei de Souza	Faculdade de Tecnologia de Indaiatuba, São Paulo
John Trimbur	Worcester Polytechnic Institute
Christopher Wilkey	Northern Kentucky University

COMMUNITY LITERACY Journal

Editors	Michael R. Moore DePaul University
	John Warnock University of Arizona
Senior Assistant Editor	Amanda Gaddam DePaul University
Journal Manager	Daniel James Carroll DePaul University
Copyeditors	Dana Dunham DePaul University
	Tricia Hermes DePaul University
	Kendall Steinle DePaul University
Design & Production Editor	Kimberly Coon DePaul University
Book & New Media Review Editor	Jim Bowman St. John Fisher College
Social Media Editor	Melissa Pompos University of Central Florida
Consulting Editors	Eric Plattner DePaul University
	Stephanie Vie Fort Lewis College
	Rachael Wendler Univerity of Arizona

Submissions

The peer-reviewed *Community Literacy Journal* seeks contributions for upcoming issues. We welcome submissions that address social, cultural, rhetorical, or institutional aspects of community literacy; we particularly welcome pieces authored in collaboration with community partners.

Manuscripts should be submitted according to the standards of the *MLA Handbook for Writers of Research Papers*, 7th ed. (New York: MLA).

Shorter and longer pieces are acceptable (8–25 manuscript pages) depending on authors' approaches. Case studies, reflective pieces, scholarly articles, etc., are all welcome.

To submit manuscripts, visit our site—communityliteracy.org—and register as an author. Send queries to Michael Moore: mmoore46@depaul.edu.

Advertising

The Community Literacy Journal welcomes advertising. The journal is published twice annually, in the Fall and Spring (Nov. and Mar.). Deadlines for advertising are two months prior to publication (Sept. and Jan.).

Ad Sizes and Pricing

Half page (trim size 6X4.5)	$200
Full page (trim size 6X9)	$350
Inside back cover (trim size 6X9)	$500
Inside front cover (trim size 6X9)	$600

Format

We accept .PDF, .JPG, .TIF or .EPS. All advertising images should be camera-ready and have a resolution of 300 dpi. For more information, please contact the Design & Production Editor at kimberly.coon@gmail.com.

Copyright © 2013 Community Literacy Journal
ISSN 1555-9734

Community Literacy Journal is a member of the Council of Editors of Learned Journals.

Printing and distribution managed by Parlor Press.

ized 2013

COMMUNITY LITERACY Journal

Volume 7 Issue 2 Spring 2013

Table of Contents

Articles

La Hermandad and Chicanas Organizing: The Community Rhetoric of the *Comisión Femenil Mexicana Nacional* 1
Kendall Leon

Becoming Qualified to Teach Low-literate Refugees: A Case Study of One Volunteer Instructor 21
Kristen H. Perry

Literacy as an Act of Creative Resistance: Joining the Work of Incarcerated Teaching Artists at a Maximum-Security Prison 39
Anna Plemons

Constructing Adult Literacies at a Local Literacy Tutor-Training Program 53
Ryan Roderick

A Place for Ecopedagogy in Community Literacy 77
Rhonda Davis

Book and New Media Reviews

From the Review Desk 93
Jim Bowman

Keywords: Refugee Literacy 95
Michael MacDonald

Writing from These Roots: Literacy in a Hmong-American Community 101
Reviewed by Abigail L. Montgomery

Affirming Students' Right to Their Own Language: Bridging Language Policies and Pedagogical Practice 105
Reviewed by Leah Durán

Writing in Rhythm: Spoken Word Poetry in Urban Classrooms and
Youth Poets: Empowering Literacies In and Out of Schools 109
Reviewed by Lance Langdon

*The Hard Work of Imagining: The Inaugural Summit of the National
Consortium of Writing Across Communities* 115
Reviewed by Brian Hendrickson

La Hermandad and Chicanas Organizing: The Community Rhetoric of the *Comisión Femenil Mexicana Nacional*

Kendall Leon

To address the need for situated accounts of community rhetoric, this article examines the legacy of the first Chicana feminist organization, the *Comisión Femenil Mexicana Nacional (CFMN)*. The *CFMN* and their archival collection provide[d] Chicanas an education about how to interpret, be and act in the world. To invent a rhetorical identity, and an organization that makes change, the *CFMN* 1) invoked a remembering of a Chicana history of policy making to incite other Chicanas into political action, and 2) strategically drew on the use of the Chicana concept of *"La Hermandad"* to define a particular Chicana method of collectivity.

Chicana writer and activist Cherríe Moraga aptly writes, "Ironically, the most 'universal work'—writing capable of reaching the hearts of the greatest number of people—is the most culturally specific" (*Last Generation* 291). Likewise, our field's popular conceptualization of community rhetoric—that is, the theory and practice of being in and making communities—has operated on a notion that what has been treated as canonical is both universal and comprehensive. In other words, "community" has become the stabilized term of choice to indicate a rhetorical collectivity. For cultural and political reasons, the methods and discourse through which we organize and affiliate often emerge from something that is shared—whether that is geographic proximity, language systems, "visible" difference, or histories and memories. What we need more of are actual accounts of what this process of affiliation looks like when it happens, especially for those of us who have been typically been marked as the visible "other" in community based scholarship[1].

In a 2011 special issue of *Reflections* on African American Contributions to Community Literacy, editor David Green reaffirms the importance of "pay[ing] attention to the way people deploy literacy in communal settings to resist, negotiate, transform, and make sense of the power relations they experience" (2). Often, as Green points out, how to "deploy literacy" for strategic ends is learned in the "community classroom," particularly for groups who have been historically excluded from institutional spaces (6). As such, Green advocates for these spaces, like community organizations, to receive "more attention for the type of pedagogical training they provide" (6). Similarly, Terese Monberg researches the rhetorical practices of the Filipino American National Historical Society (FANHS) organization. According to Monberg, FAHNS creates a "rhetorical space" for Filipina/o Americans to uncover and share histories, writing, memories, and to negotiate relationships with each other, and a larger American culture—and much of this work would go unnoticed using typical methodologies that focus on public texts (87-8).

To address the need for situated accounts of community rhetoric, and of community organizations as a site for "pedagogical training," I turn to my archival research on one of the first Chicana activist organizations, the *Comisión Femenil Mexicana Nacional* (*CFMN*). While they were an active organization, the *CFMN* —and later, their archival collection—provide[d] Chicanas an education about how to interpret, be and act in the world. Their practices were used to instantiate an organizing Chicana, which in turn, enabled an effectual organization (the *CFMN*) and a Chicana movement. Utilizing theory in the flesh as a methodological heuristic to analyze documents contained in the *CFMN* archival collection, in my larger research project I examine the way the Chicanas[2] of the *CFMN* use[d] experience to make things such as community organizations, textual histories and practices.

My focus for this particular article centers on these Chicanas' rhetorical moves to make organizing and collectivity part of what it means to be a Chicana, and thusly, to enable change. This is especially relevant given that Chicana emerges in response to a shared experience by Latin@s and/or Mexican@s of being treated as a-rhetorical. To achieve the invention of a rhetorical identity and an organization that makes change, Chicanas of the *CFMN* 1) invoked a remembering of a Chicana history of policy making to incite other Chicanas into political action; and 2) strategically drew on the use of the Chicana concept of "*La Hermandad*" (Chicana sisterhood) to define a particular Chicana method of collectivity. In writing this article, I want to contribute to the existent scholarship in community literacy by offering a situated account of communities and their organizing practices by examining the strategic practices employed by the Chicanas of the *CFMN* as evidenced in their archival documents.

About the *Comisión Femenil Mexicana Nacional*

The idea for a Chicana feminist organization originated at the 1970 *National Chicano Issues Conference*, when a group of Chicanas at the conference felt that that the Chicano leaders at the conference were not addressing their needs or concerns. In response, these women physically left and met separately. It was at this meeting they drafted the following series of resolutions, which would become the textual framework for the *CFMN*. In one draft of their forming resolutions, the *CFMN* pointed to a dissonance between the experience of being constructed by Chicanos as not leaders, and the reality that they were active and organizing. In the document "Resolution Adopted by the Women's Workshop 10/10/70 Sacramento, California; [A]Proposal for a Comision Femenil Mexicana," the *CFMN* leaders wrote:

> The effort and work of the Chicana/Mexicana women in the Chicano movement is generally obscured because women are not accepted as community leaders either by the Chicano movement or by the Anglo establishment.
>
> The existing myopic attitude does not, however, prove that women are not able to participate. It does not prove that women are not active, indispensable (representing over 50% of the population), experienced and

knowledgeable in organizational, tactical and strategic aspects of a people's movement.

THEREFORE, in order to terminate exclusion of female leadership in the Chicano/Mexican movement and in the community, be it

RESOLVED, that a Chicana/Mexican Women's Commission be established at this conference which will represent women in all areas where Mexicans prevail.

This literacy event—the drafting of a series of resolutions—documented an exigency for an organization that would make visible the problems and issues particular to Chicana women, as well as provide an avenue for Chicana leadership development. Following this initial drafting of resolutions, in 1973 the Chicanas involved with the initial formation of the *CFMN* organized a conference in Goleta, California for Chicana women. It was at this conference that the *CFMN* became an official organization: by laws were passed and leaders were elected[3].

Since their inception, the *CFMN* became one of the first and most influential Chicana feminist organizations. While their role as an activist organization dwindled in the 1990s, they continued to serve as a philanthropic and leadership development organization well into the mid 2000s. Many of the ideological arguments produced by this organization as well as the documents themselves served as foundational texts for the Chicana movement, and are later reproduced and used to invent what it means to be a Chicana[4]. In addition to the *Comisión* national board, there were over twenty active chapter organizations formed that focused on regional and local concerns as representatives of the CFMN[5]. During the over 30 year span of the organization's lifetime, the relationship between the chapter organizations and the national board was a source of confusion and at times, disruption, in the organization's formation. Underlying their organization's history was a tension between the chapters and the *CFMN* (the national organization), which was partly constituted by differences in localized goals and in the expectations for the relationship between the national board and the individual chapters[6]. Based on the contents of the archival collection, a considerable amount of time and materials were spent determining the relationship. For example, the *CFMN* structure was outlined at multiple moments, with varying relationships established between the chapters and the national board. Figure 1: Copy of an Organizational Chart, demonstrates one of many attempts by the CFMN to put in print the administrative work flow between the national board of directors, the chapter representatives and its various committees. In this version, the chapter representatives appear to be an offshoort of the national board of directors.

Leading up to a 1984 *CFMN* retreat primarily devoted to discussing this relationship, the *CFMN* sent a questionnaire to the local chapters inquiring about the role of *CFMN* in relation to the chapters and what the chapters wanted from the national board. The responses ranged from wanting the *CFMN* to be "a quasi dictatorship while concentrating on developing our infrastructure" to facilitating more opportunities for the chapters to meet and giving each chapter more recognition, as well as "... mostly to be left alone" ("CFMN Questionnaire")[7]. The retreat then was organized to

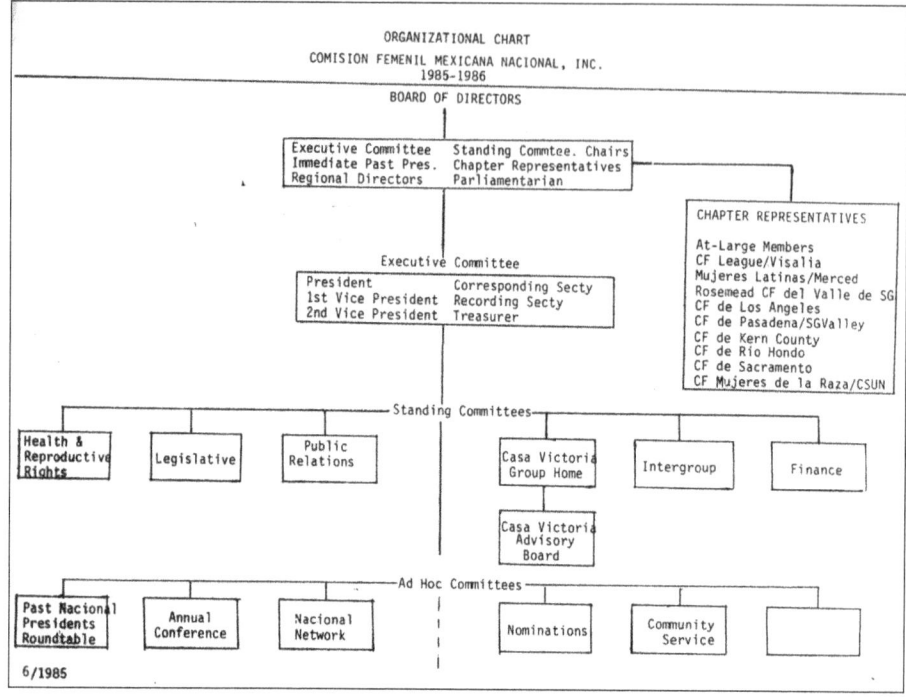

Figure 1. Copy of an Organizational Chart

address these concerns and "determine accountability and commitment of chapters to CFMN and vis-versa [sic]" ("CFMN Retreat"). While admittedly distinct from the national organization in terms of practices or concerns, the chapters fell under the scope of the *CFMN* because of a recognition that their members shared a history and goal.

Undeniably, the impact of the *CFMN*'s organizing efforts is widespread geographically and chronologically. Respective to our field's concerns with texts, the *CFMN* served as an amasser and disseminator of information and writings on Chicana related issues, which included writing and circulating a widely read newsletter (the *CFM* newsletter). The *CFMN*'s written testimonies, newsletter articles and activist writings are anthologized and referenced in Chicana studies[8]. As part of the California Ethnic and Minority Archives housed at the UC Santa Barbara and UCLA libraries, their extensive archival collection documents not only their involvement in the Chicana movement, but serves as a record of the movement and of the Civil Rights era in general. Their collection also includes the writings of other organizations, and information about various pertinent policies, measures and issues. In addition to the textual impact of the organization, the leaders of the *CFMN* also formed two offshoot organizations: the Chicana Service Action Center (a Chicana employment and education resource center), and El Centro de Niños (a bilingual childcare center)[9]. Another primary goal of the *CFMN* was to provide leadership development for Chicanas, particularly within the public sphere. Toward this end, several of the *CFMN* leaders went on to lead accomplished public careers; most notably, former *CFMN* president Gloria Molina, was elected to the California State Assembly in 1982.

As an activist organization, they are also well known amongst Chicanas and non-Chicanas for their participation in the cause to stop a Los Angeles county hospital from routinely performing involuntary sterilizations of Mexican women. The *CFMN* were co-plaintiffs in the landmark case Madrigal v. Quilligan in 1975 against the doctors who were culpable of compulsory sterilization[10]. Although the judge ruled in favor of the doctors, their participation in the case garnered the *CFMN* notoriety and influence on Chicana matters in politics: leaders of the *CFMN* were frequently called upon to present testimonies on public issues such as the Equal Rights Amendment, access to education employment training, and pro-choice advocacy[11].

Because they were increasingly called upon to present "expert" testimony on behalf of the Chicana community, in one of their audio-recorded meeting minutes, the *CFMN* board members had a debate about setting standards and criteria for such testimonies in part to ensure that what they were speaking on should be considered a Chicana issue, and also what their take on such issues *as Chicanas* should be ("Board of Directors Meeting"). Thusly, in addition to their work within the public realm—work that might look more familiar and commonly studied in Rhetoric and Composition—the *CFMN* also contributed internally to the Chicana community, and to the making of Chicana identity. In the early stages of this project, it was because of their well-known orators and their involvement in highly publicized cases that I became interested in the *CFMN*. As I began my research though, my particular interest shifted elsewhere. I redirected my attention to the very fact that they were and are an organization instead of individual people. This is an organization that accomplished, among other things, significant documentation of their growth as a Chicana organization and what that meant for themselves and for other Chicanas. I noticed the prolific notes and cards, nestled alongside their programmatic writing, from people wanting to know the *CFMN*'s opinions on matters.

Turning to the *CFMN* for direction on how to be and act became clear at an early *CFMN* retreat on September 23, 1973 in California. At the retreat, board members asked attendees to respond to the following question: "what role would you like facilitators to take". The two choices were: "a) deal with the inter-personal relationships involved in working in an organization b) working with a group regarding sensitivity and self-awareness as Chicanas." The majority of the responses were "both." At the bottom of one of the responses an attendee went so far as to note: "Don't like facilitators to ask questions. Would prefer them to make statements" ("Comisión Femenil Retreat 1973"). As we can see, Chicanas associated with the *CFMN* wanted guidance from the leadership on how to work as an organization and how to be as a Chicana. Through their extensive archiving practices, their contribution to the making of Chicana in the collective continues. What became especially interesting to notice is the way that the members of the organization understood Chicana identity to mediate what they could (and should) do as an organization; in this way, Chicana shaped the rhetorical practices of the organization.

Studying the *CFMN* then for community literacy scholars is especially salient. The *CFMN* operated at the intersections of identity and collectivity as both emergent from shared experience as well as mediating how then to respond to such conditions[12]. This responsive emergence in tandem with a correlative response is part of what also constitutes a theoretical tradition arguably born from Chicanadad, and which was used as my methodological apparatus: theory in the flesh.

Methodological Underpinnings: Theorizing from/about Experience

In her short introductory essay for a section in the edited collection *This Bridge Called My Back*, Cherríe Moraga develops a theory of identity that stems from lived experiences from which a "politic" is built: "A theory in the flesh means one where the physical realities of our lives . . . all fuse to create a politic born out of necessity" (23). Theory in the flesh is thusly recognition of our lived experience, which includes the way that we are articulated given the skin and positionality we inhabit. In my research, I adopt theory in the flesh as a empirical theory of existence that works in tandem and tension with a correlative action: "Our strategy is how we cope—how we measure and weigh what is to be said and when, what is to be done and how, and to whom and to whom, daily deciding/risking who it is we can call an ally, call a friend (whatever that person's skin, sex, or sexuality)" ("I Have Dreamed of a Bridge" xix). Despite what might be the painful experiences we encounter as women of color, Moraga asks us to consider our rhetorical ability to read our experiences alongside others and to connect as a strategy for survival. Theory in the flesh involves recognizing our lived experiences and coming to a critical consciousness about this, coupled with our responses, or actions to alter the worlds that produce such conditions.

Theory in the flesh has been extended by post positivist realists who further make the connection between identity and a physical reality that while subject mediated, is *real* (see for example *Martín-Alcoff; Martín-Alcoff and Mohanty;* Moya). Post positivist realists understand identity not as limitless or limiting, but rather as mediating yet grounded; and more importantly, as epistemic. Paula Moya argues that it "is precisely because identities have a referential relationship to the world that they are politically and epistemically important: indeed, identities instantiate the links between individuals and groups and central organizing principles of our society" (*Learning*, 13).

In other words, as community literacy scholars, we should be studying identity, and in particular Chicana identity, because it connects people and incites us to action. According to several intake surveys of the *CFMN*'s membership, when asked what they hoped to gain from involvement in the *Comisión* and secondarily, what the *Comisión* should do for its members, many of the responses centered on establishing relationships with other Chicanas:

- "It is important to meet and interact with other Latinas,"
- "..keep me informed of Chicana issues & how to be involved in these issues and how to mentor other Chicanas..."
- "I needed to relate to other women with initiative, be an active network and support system to fall back on; wanted to become active member in such an organization for Chicanas, to provide a supportive and encouraging environment where I can be with other Latinas..."
- "..because I wanted to meet other Latinas and be able to learn from others as well as to share my knowledge; to become more involved in community activities and to be more aware of my culture.."

- "I did volunteer work at NOW and noticed one summer and I saw there was a noticeable lack of contact with the Chicana community so I looked up Chicana organizations and decided to join…"
- "..allow me to work with other like-minded women on projects, campaigns, etc which benefit the Latina and her community, seeking a means by which I can utilize my energies in constructive ways.."
- "to have an impact in my community and not be so isolated from it.."

(CSAC, "Mexican/Chicana Women's Survey")

Tellingly, many of these responses demonstrate both an expectation that a Chicana organization would serve to create and maintain relationships between Chicanas. At the same time, this expectation incited people to join and participate in this organization. The sentiments conveyed in this list also indicate that a primary purpose of the *CFMN* as a Chicana organization was definitional. For instance, in the quote in the second bullet point, the prospective *CFMN* member stated that she was interested in joining in order to "keep me informed of Chicana issues & how to be involved in these issues and how to mentor other Chicanas…" It was through affiliation with this organization that people hoped to find out what was important for Chicanas, how to act and ostensibly, how to treat people. Affiliation to this identity then mediated even day-to-day actions. As I will later discuss, part of this mediation involved changing the methods for activist practices. Chicana identity and its relationship to the formation of communities is especially salient precisely because Chicana is a constructed identity that reflects and refracts a material existence.

On the Term "Chicana"

Scholars have argued about who or what is included in the domain of Chicano or Latino (see for example Grosfoguel et al). Some of these names explicitly center culture within the colonial moment—such as "Hispanic" or even "Latin American" (Mignolo). This tension in names and naming is evident throughout the textual artifacts that I examined produced by various members of the *Comisión*. For example, on speeches, resolutions and meeting minutes I read hand written notes on the documents that changed Chicana to "Latina"—or visa versa—based on the rhetorical purpose of the document, or if the author felt the term violated the concept of *la hermandad* governing the organization and its practices.

Undoubtedly, "Chicano/a" is a rhetorical and intentional term. Chicano/a people created "Chicano" identity to speak to the experiences of living in the United States, with a connection to a Latino/a background, and for most, recognizing an indigenous affiliation as well.[13] Chicano/a then acknowledges a mixed blood and cultural background— a reclamation in the face of a society that privileges mythic "purity." Foundational to the Chicano movement is a productive nostalgia for a pre-conquest Atzlán as a response to a literal and metaphoric displacement from our homelands[14]. Chicano also has historical and contemporary connections with the United Farm Workers (UFW) movement, with its initiation as an independent organization in 1962 often serving as origin moment of the national Chicano movement. As with any "origin" story, the Chicano movement is constellative. Interwoven with the UFW political struggles, including the well-known national boycott of grapes, other activist organizations and actions emerge. Alongside these emergences, the Chicano movement also began within academia, with Rodolfo Acuña teaching the first Mexican American history class in 1966. Chicano therefore connotes an activist and oppositional identity (Castañeda; for criticism of this narrative see Pérez *Decolonial Imaginary*).

Chicana was developed to identify the particular gendered experiences of women, which the Chicano movement was criticized for forgetting, or only admitting to service Chicanos as helpmates. For those who identify as Chicana, the degree of tangential relation to the Chicano movement varies. Likewise, the Chicana movement is treated as distinct from the predominately Anglo-centric feminist movement as being historically unable to address the particular concerns of women of color. But again, any relation to the feminist movement varies for each Chicana. In addition to Chicana as emerging or responding tangentially to other movements, there are frequently similar origin stories for Chicana identity as a distinct identity. For example, Chicanas often point to Chicana literature as pivotal to Chicana identity and to the Chicana movement broadly. In her edited "collection," the *Chicana Cultural Studies Forum*, Angie Chabram-Dernersesian interviewed well known scholars in Chicano and Chicana studies about the relation to Chican@ studies and cultural studies. Many of the Chicanas in the forum mention the edited collection *This Bridge Called My Back* as foundational to their own identities and to Chicana studies in general. The writings of Ana Castillo, Cherríe Moraga, and Gloria Anzaldúa, among others, are referenced as pivotal to what it means to be a Chicana.

While both theory and the flesh and its offshoot post positivist realism understand identity to be connective and grounded in reality that can be articulated and read through writing, the emphasis thus far has been on literary writing. In my following case study of the *Comisión Femenil Mexicana Nacional Organization*, I extend the reading of the reality and epistemic of identity in the programmatic writing of an organization.

Chicanas Inventing Histories and/of *Reglas* in the Archives

People like organizations, rivers, mountains and valleys, all have their beginnings, their turns, their ups and their downs. However, one characteristic common to all things physical, is that they leave their mark in spite of the changes which occur over the years.
Francisca Flores, "Chicana Service Action Center"

As scholars of color know, history matters. It matters a great deal for those of us whose histories are often constructed for us. And it matters even more for Chicanas as it is a "contemporary" identity and thusly, histories must be invented and re-remembered[15]. Change, according to Chicana historian Emma Pérez, "is formed discursively, in the past, by the present" (32). The ownership over the making of a history— of cataloging experiences and the emergence of Chicana activist identity and its effects on action—is one way that history and historicizing is part of a Chicana community rhetoric both in terms of what is valued and what is practiced. The attention given to the creation of their archival collection and the level of documentation the *CFMN* included in their archival files demonstrates that history for Chicanas matters a great deal. History of course matters for everyone, but as we see, part of claiming a Chicana identity means that you are aware of a history, claim an affiliation to it, and commit to sharing and teaching histories. Such an experience for those of us who are constructed as a-rhetorical or ineffectual becomes the fodder through which we invent, remember and organize our communities. Chicanas understand that their interventions in history mediate present and future positionalities and their associative rhetorical actions. Chicanas had (and have) to invent histories of organizing as part of their subjectivity; in this way we see that the contemporary identity of Chicana is an epistemic for the creation of histories.

Returning to the introduction of the *CFMN*'s founding resolutions, the organization emerged as a response to not being treated as "experienced and knowledgeable in organizational, tactical and strategic aspects of a people's movement" ("Resolution"). Therefore, the *CFMN* understood that part of their role as an organization was to be just that. But, I must point out that they were not saying in the resolutions they drafted that they have to *become* these things. Rather, they indicated that they were *already* knowledgeable about organizing. The problem they identify is that this history and their current activism were not being recognized. What the *CFMN* did was to remind their members that Chicanas were always organizing.

While part of Chicana identity is to be responsive and to incite change, this happens in dialogue with a past that has either been forgotten or misread. Therefore, the Chicanas of the *CFMN* incorporated history to legitimize activism and its purposes. More often than not what this looked like was using histories of Mexican American women as precedents for activism. The purpose was to demonstrate to other Chicanas that their concerns and involvement were both warranted and, in fact, part of what it means to be a Chicana. Several examples of the strategic use of history can be found in the documents contained in the *CFMN* archival collection that demonstrate Chicanas turning to a forgotten history of active women to create a productive lineage with contemporary Chicanas. Some of this remembering took place in the rhetorical moment; others took place in the recounting of these events as an interpretive framework. For instance, in "The Woman of La Raza[16]," Enriqueta Longauex y Vásquez reads a Raza conference through a history of women who have been active, but were often overlooked when recounting the history of revolutionizing:

> While attending a Raza conference in Colorado this year, I went to one of the workshops that were held to discuss the role of the Chicana woman. When the time came for the woman to make the presentation to the full conference, the only thing that the workshop representative said was this: 'It was the consensus of the group that the Chicana woman does not want to be liberated' . . . Surely we could have at least come up with something to add to that statement. I sat back and thought, why? Why? . . .Looking at our history, I can see why this would be true. The role of the Chicana woman has been a very strong one, although a silent one. (1)

In this recollection of Raza conference, Longauex y Vásquez uses history as a way to understand her experiences at the conference in Colorado that lead a presenter to claim that the "Chicana woman" does not want liberation. As a response, Longauex y Vásquez then *uses* history to subtly support while at the same time question the actions taken given the history of Chicana women in the revolution in Mexico.

> When the woman has seen the suffering of her people she has always responded bravely and as a totally committed and equal human. My mother told me of how, during the time of Pancho Villa and the revolution in Mexico, she saw the men march through the village continually for three days and then she saw the battalion of woman [sic] marching for a whole day. The woman [sic] carried food and supplies; also, they were fully armed wearing loaded 'carrilleras.' In battle they fought alongside the men. Out of the Mexican Revolution came the revolutionary personage 'Adelita,' who wore rebozo crossed at the bosom as a symbol of revolutionary woman [sic] in Mexico[17]. (1)

The implications for this narration are that women have always fought "alongside men" and perhaps this is the reason why Chicana women do "not need to be liberated"; we have always been equals, and the problem is that we have forgotten our history. The purpose then was to remember this lineage.

Likewise, in an article about the *CFMN*, "La Chicana Organizes: The *Comisión Femenil Mexicana* in Perspective," Gema Matsuda narrates a lineage of Mexican women as active contributors in and to histories. This lineage is used not only as a heuristic to interpret the *CFMN* as an organization. Matsuda also then locates the *CFMN*'s leaders as part of this history of women who make change:

> Recorded history of the Mexican woman goes as far back as the Indians who first populated our continent. In Chichén-Itzá Mayan gods were appeased with the lives of young maidens. And many scholars agree that the conquest of México City by Cortéz was possible only because of the invaluable help of La Malinche. At first glance, one may not see the connection between the above named incidents because the lesson learned is a philosophic rather than historical one…The importance of the women in both of these cases was of a crucial, if not indispensable, nature. Their contribution to history extends beyond their recognized role as child bearers" (25).

In this opening Matsuda begins by demonstrating that Mexican women have played an instrumental role in shaping history, but this role "at first glance" may not be recognized or recognizable. Matsuda then traced the involvement of Mexican women/Chicana women, noting names of leaders in historical struggles, leading to "a few women who have risen above the type-casting to which we are all subjected and have become valuable leaders of the [Chicano] movement" (26). A pivotal move in this recounting happens next.

After demonstrating that Mexican women contributed to change in history that has not been recognized, Matsuda uses this illuminated history as a way to both establish the exigency for the *CFMN*, and to place the leaders of the *CFMN* as part of this history as agents of change. As such, Matsuda's narrative turns to an introduction of Francisca Flores, one of the founders of the *CFMN*. Matsuda specifically describes Flores as an interventionist, responding to and altering the cultural frameworks that were preventing Chicanas from seeing themselves as effectual:

> Francisca Flores saw this problem and recognized the cultural trends which perpetuate it—maternal overprotection, male chauvinism, lack of incentive for female higher education, and, by extension, lack of Chicanas in the professional fields. With the purpose of combating these very problems, she and other women who, like her, had learned the art of organizing got together in order to discuss the feasibility of forming an organization which would promote Chicanas in all professions. ("La Chicana" 25)

In this case, Matsuda narrated the historical involvement of Mexican and Chicana women that serves to establish a legacy to the *CFMN*'s endeavors; Flores in turn becomes part of that historical legacy. The strategy to remind audiences of a historical legacy that the *CFMN*'s leaders were building upon garnered a type of legitimacy for the leaders, and for the Chicana movement more broadly. It normalized activist practices as a way to compose Chicana subjectivity as always already effectual, or rhetorical.

For the *CFMN*, a legacy of being active and resistant had to also coalesce with organizing and being organized. As Gloria Anzaldúa writes: "…the new mestiza copes by developing a tolerance for contradictions, a tolerance for ambiguity. She learns to be an Indian in Mexican culture, to be Mexican from an Anglo point of view. She learns to juggle cultures. She has a plural personality, she operates in a pluralistic mode" (*Borderlands*, 80). Mestiza, and by association, Chicana, is grounded in the ability to operate at a contradictory nexus. This framework can also be applied to the *CFMN* organization.

In a paper written for a Mexican Literature class on the 1973 *CFMN* conference in Goleta, which is included in the *CFMN* archival collection, attendee Amelia Lorenzo Wilson reflects on the purpose of the gathering: "The first convention of CFM Nacional, Inc was held June 2nd and 3rd in Goleta, California, with the implied purposes of building a strong Mexican women's organization. It was considered imperative by the founders of CFM that such an organization would demonstrate that the Chicanas had finally discovered a need for an identity and a willingness to express confidence in her ideals" (2). Lorenzo Wilson comments though that this purpose was lost amidst a disconnect between the need for organizing principles with the desire for activism:

> The convention organizers took an authoritarian-defensive stand in the attempt to preserve "Roberts Rules" to try to stay on the main line brought out some very important disputes that practically destroyed the convention [. . .] For the majority of participants it was the first immersion in parliamentary procedures and a cold bath it proved to be [. . .] Without generalizing too much, camps formed almost from the start. The organizers and founders of La Comisión [. .] justly wished to protect the three years' work that had brought them to the point of founding a national organization. Another camp—composed of a varied age group, but basically younger and nosier—were interested in ideology and vastly

impatient with the bureaucratic slowness inherent in any organization. (3 of 6)

The nature of being an organization necessitates that it achieves stability often through rules or routine procedures. As an organization that was based on an identity of resistance, the *CFMN* had to presumably operate as a contradiction. Throughout the *CFMN*'s 30-year history, the extent to which the *CFMN* should adopt rules and regulations as an organization without going against the premises of Chicana identity remained a source of contention. In an article for their newsletter, the *CFM Report*, the CFMN board members reflect upon less than productive meetings in which the organization "has been split and the sessions 'busted' so there was natural concern, that some present were there to break rather than build" ("The Experience 1). The meetings were divided because of the contention between the board, who wanted to adhere to organizing techniques like Roberts Rules of Orders, and other members who saw these organizational practices as at odds with being a Chicana activist as they "claim that rules and parliamentary procedure is the 'man' bag" (1). However, in the CFM report, the authors—presumably the *CFMN* board members—respond that "[t]his claim, although used very successfully to divide meetings of Mexican Americans and Chicanos, time and again, is false, because Mexicans and Mexican organizations have their 'reglas' and know how to use them when someone does not observe them. So, rules and procedures, by-laws and constitutions are not the exclusive property of the 'white man.'" (1) Instead, the opponents to *reglas* "still have not learned the history of the movements or of their own people" (1). To conceptualize Chicana activism as legitimately achieved through organizational practice, the authors of the *CFM* report instantiated organizing into a pre-colonial history:

> The Aztecs had their judicial system and their order to their society. They had a system of laws. And the Spanish came along with theirs, so the Mexicans have a longer history of parliamentary procedures than do the Anglos of the United States. As a matter of fact, from the Spain, whose law dates back to Roman law, we have a longer history in this respect than does the 'melted pot American.' Young people, and some of the older folks should learn their history and quit falling for the wrong 'cliché' such as the 'white man's bag' because we have a longer history or can compare our history with anyone else's on any aspect of social organization, etc. ("The Experience" 1)

As evidenced in the above excerpt about the tense meeting, problems arose when Chicanas forgot a pre-colonial history of "reglas." Having such rules is what enables the continuity of organization, and the ability to act. As the above article notes, such divisiveness within the organization planning sessions "busted" up planning meetings; it appeared that people were intent on breaking rather than building. In response then, seemingly to "build," the article reminds the *CFMN* members, who may in fact have been the people mentioned in this article, that the Aztecs, and the Spanish, had rules before the colonizers ever came. Remembering a history of rules and regulations here is used by the *CFMN* to redress divisive actions. The *CFMN* leaders intervened in an idea of history that some Chicanas held that *reglas* were only part of the "white man's bag" which rendered themselves as not part of a legacy of rule makers in order produce a construction of Mexicans as organizing. The *CFMN* leaders do this to make organizing part of the repertoire of Chicana identity and rhetoric. This is likewise achieved materially through the creation of objects like their archival collections as a mechanism through which community is further built between generations, whereby lessons and evidence of Chicana organizing are remembered. Not only did the *CFMN* leaders instill organizing as part of the habituations of being a Chicana, but they also documented a method of organizing particular to Chicana identity: the concept of *La Hermandad*.

Collective Practices and *La Hermandad*

La Hermandad is a concept of Chicana sisterhood employed by the *CFMN* as reflective of how Chicanas organize. It is also used at times to produce Chicana organizational practice. In an article for *Encuentro Femenil*[18], *CFMN* leader Francisca Flores reflected on the production and subsequent impact of *La Hermandad* as produced at the 1973 Chicana national conference in Goleta:

> Chicanas expressed a dire need to establish a national means of communication among women. This communication system would strengthen a new feeling of '*Hermandad*' (sisterhood) among Chicanas. This communication system and the new philosophy of *hermandad* would motivate Chicanas to identify, understand and work against the racist and sexist economic social forces adversely affecting the Chicana and her people. (Italics in the original, "Chicana Service Action Center" 5)

Note that the philosophy of *hermandad* is described as inciting change in Chicanas and Chicana activist practice. This philosophy and way of communicating is responsive to outside forces yet inwardly focused in its production and employment. For the *CFMN*, this concept is used most frequently to redress and then redirect action.

One example is in a response to a series of memos amongst members regarding tension between the members of the national board and chapter leaders. The memos decried member behavior that is seen as antithetical to connectedness and as unsupportive of the *CFMN*, and by association, the Chicana movement in general, which included disrupting meetings and negative talk about the Board and its particular leaders. In one memo written by a past president (Christine Fuentes) and circulated amongst its membership and chapter organization, Fuentes reminds the *CFMN* members that the organization's foundations were:

> …built on such concepts as unity, goodwill and *hermandad*. Achieving these goals calls for a tremendous amount of work and dedication from all members. Obviously this cannot be accomplished if the present leadership elects instead to focus its energies on the negative…One cannot help, but question the leadership capabilities and moral judgment of a Board displaying conduct, which is divisive and alienating. At a time when unity is imperative for success, Comision members must insist

on being guided by a Board sensitive and responsive to the needs of all Chicanas. Let us seek to work together in constructive and positive ways. Comision's survival is dependant on this.

Within the archival collection, this memo is included in the "Administrative" files, which highlights its importance as an organizing mechanism. What the record of Fuentes's redress indicates is that adherence to *hermandad* is used to question the actions of its members and its boards whenever they appeared to not be positive or constructive. In other words, to be a Chicana [organization] means that one does not operate through negative behavior; rather, its actions should be productive and in the spirit of building community.

Not only did the *CFMN* use *la hermandad* to help define what it meant to be a Chicana organization, it was also used to redirect action. In a follow up memo to Fuentes regarding the behavior of the *CFMN* board, the Pasadena chapter of the organization wrote to *CFMN* president Gloria Moreno-Wycoff to convey their disappointment in the circulated memos, primarily because *La Comisión* should be dedicated to promoting Chicanas and their welfare:

> Should not such a sensitive information be dealth [sic] with by the CFMN board in a more discreet manner? 2. Are we (Comisión) not as a whole supportive of all our members and does not the letter make reference to the CFMN taking action against one of our sisters? 3. Does sending out such letter suggest that the CFMN Board cannot handled [sic] its private matters? 4. In its accusations, it not the letter somewhat slanderous to one of our members reputation? 5. Are we as Chicana women striving for all Chicana women not contradicting ourselves by attacking one of our own? ("Memo to Gloria Moreno Wycoff")

The understanding that Chicana identification implied a shared commitment to *la hermandad* became a lens through which the activists interpreted and altered their actions. This sentiment to redirect activist efforts reflected the understanding that Chicana action should operate on the unit of the community. The invocation of their commitment to sisterhood, which was sent out via the above memo to the organization, served to shift, or perhaps remind the organization members of the way that Chicanas should be: in essence, reestablishing its epistemology. This makes sense given that Chicana identity is one that specifically emerges as a response to conditions in which one is marked as *not* productive. As a result then of being compelled into a position of non-action, Chicana identity emerges as a position of action; more specifically, a particular type of action that not only builds on experience, but is instantiated each time that *la hermandad* is invoked. Therefore, through its invocation of this concept, it can be assumed that the *CFMN* hoped that *la hermandad* would become a habituated practice of its members, and by association, of those who affiliate as Chicana. *La hermandad* becomes then part of the positionality of Chicana as built from the flesh. It serves as heuristic through which Chicanas view change or the purpose of their work[19]. Through examining the use of *la hermandad* to produce activist practice, we can see how these particular habituations are realized collectively.

Implications

As a response to the need for more situated accounts of community organizations as sites for education, I traced the specific practices employed by the *CFMN* to make a Chicana feminist organization. In doing so, this article has demonstrated that studying the rhetoric of marginalized groups—marginalized in politics, in publics, and in research that studies "communities"—can teach us about the different ways that people might affiliate, and how that affiliation can be used to make change. While *la hermandad* was used to redirect and alter the actions of members that were seen as violating part of their Chicana identity, to be a successful organization and by association, an effectual organization, the *CFMN* had to productively invent—or rather, remember— their legacy of organizing. In this way, we see that claiming one is a Chicana carries explicit political implications that mediate performances of what it means to be a Chicana—and by association, what it means to be a Chicana organization. At the same time, Chicana is a rhetoric that is emergent from experience in so far as those who affiliate as such tend to share similar experiential knowledge, which we might say constitutes a "community." Arguably, this community has been created and sustained in and through literacy artifacts. For Chicanas the focus has often been on poetic texts, but as I have demonstrated, the making of Chicana identity, community organization and an associative rhetoric is also evident in programmatic and archival texts. During their tenure, the *CFMN* organization built a legacy of collective Chicana activism in the face of an experience in which being identified as Latina/Mexicana was considered to be decidedly not effectual. This legacy continued being built through the creation of an expansive archival collection of the organization, and it is rebuilt each time another Chicana learns from the *CFMN* collection what it means to be a Chicana—organized, impactful, and collective.

Endnotes

1. In particular, I am reminded of work like that of two-spirit Cherokee scholar Qwo-Li Driskill, who has written about the Cherokee concept of "duyuk'a" as a way to theorize relatedness and a harmonious balance as well as challenging our field's attention on the written word as evidence of and the mechanism through which we achieve relatedness and affiliation. Recently, Cherokee scholar Ellen Cushman has explored "gadugi", which might run parallel to our understanding of "community." While perhaps not typically published within the realm of community literacy proper, they do include discussions of rhetorical and literacy practices that emerge from shared experiences or beliefs as challenging how we define and decide on community.

2. A Note on the Use of the Term Chicana: In this article, I focus on *"Chicana"* as this is the term used by the CFMN community members. More recently, Chicanas have adopted Xicana as a way to remember and honor our indigenous heritages, as well as Chican@/Xican@ for complicating the gender identification and binary of Chicana/o.

3. For a more thorough recounting of the history of the *CFMN* and its accomplishments as a political organization, see Sonia R. García and Marisela Márquez's recent 2011 *Atzlán* article, "The *Comisión Femenil* : La Voz of a Chicana Organization"

4. See Alma García and Angie Chabram-Dernersesian for evidence of the organization's influence.

5. While the majority of these chapter organizations were in California, several were formed in Arizona, Colorado and Illinois.

6. Another point of contention expressed by the chapter organizations is geographically based. The *CFMN* collated responses to the questionnaires sent to its chapters and then used these responses to write their agenda for a board retreat. Written on the agenda under "DEFINED WHAT IS CFMN TODAY," is "Perceived as LA based" ("Retreat and Questionnaires"). This observation mirrors a general critique leveled at Chicana identity in general as it is primarily seen as affiliated with and speaking to Chicanas in California.

7. For writing researchers, it is interesting to note that several responses focused on the newsletters produced by the *CFMN* and its chapters as they equated recognition of chapters with the placement of chapter news in the national newsletter ("Retreat and Questionnaires").

8. See for example Alma García's comprehensive collection *Chicana Feminist Thought: The Basic Historical Writings*, which includes several texts written by the *CFMN* or its leaders.

9. These organizations later became independent entities.

10. Rhetoric and Composition scholar Jessica Enoch details some of the CFMN's organizing efforts against sterilization in her article "Survival Stories: Feminist Historiographic Approaches to Chicana Rhetorics of Sterilization Abuse."

11. Because they were increasingly called upon to present "expert" testimony on behalf of the Chicana community, in one of their audio recorded meeting minutes, the *CFMN* board members had a debate about setting standards and criteria for such testimonies in part to ensure that what they were speaking on should be considered a Chicana issue.

12. Similarly, Dora Ramirez Dhoore is Chicana scholar who studies tropes that have emerged within the Chicana experience and have been used for invention in a variety of creative and political works. As a type of organizing principle, in her article "Cyberborderland: Searching the Web for Xicanidad," Ramirez-Dhoore examines how the concept of mestiza Xican@s *use* mestiza consciousness to negotiate their racialized, gendered, and othered discourse." While not writing to a community literacy audience, we can see how mestiza consciousness is a concept that identifies both the shared experience of Xicanidad *and* a trope through which similarly identified people write from and to, and continue to organize around.

13. This creation of Chicano/a *by* Chicanos/as is especially important to juxtapose to other ways that groups can be made; for example, the creation of the identity and group "Hispanic" which was developed in the 1970's for the U.S. Census.

14. While this is understood to be the Aztec homeland that was taken by the United States in the Treaty of Hildago in 1848, which is now the American Southwest, Atzlán functions as more than just a literal translation to the geography.

15. Chicana literary and philosophical writers, for example, have examined and reimagined the rhetorical functions of historical figures such as *Malintzin*, *La Virgen de Guadalupe*, or *La llorona*, to reposition these *Mexicanas* as positive contributors to cultural narratives (see for example Calafell; Castillo; Gaspar de Alba).

16. This document was a column written by Vásquez for one of her columns in the Chicano newspaper, *El Grito Del Norte*. A typed copy of this without the article references was included in the *CFMN* collection.

17. The construction of Chicanas as always a part of revolutionary action is also made evident in the use of revolutionary symbols and images. For example, Figure 2 found in the *CFMN*'s archives is a very familiar image of the Chicano/a movement.

18. *Encuentro Femenil* was a Chicana feminist journal started by Chicanas such as Anna Nieto-Gómez, Adelaida R. Del Castillo, Cindy Honesto, among others. Francisca Flores (one of *CFMN*'s founders) worked closely with Nieto-Gómez. The *CFMN* also included copies of *Encuentro Femenil* in their archival collection.

19. "Alicia García," a contemporary Chicana scholar, also invokes this sense of connectedness to negotiate how she produces scholarship. She states that she questions "how much do we do as educated Chicanas that are not part of community," and, to redress this sometimes forgetting of our community ties, she "tr[ies] to use language that can be used by larger audiences." For Garcia, being a Chicana means taking the knowledge she has learned as a Mexican American in the academy and sharing it with her community (Interview).

Figure 2. Copy of a Drawing of a Chicana Revolutionary

Works Cited

Anzaldúa, Gloria. *Borderlands/La Frontera: The New Mestiza*. San Francisco, CA: Spinsters/Aunt Lute Book Company, 1987. Print.

Calafell, Bernadette Marie. "Pro(re-)claiming Loss: A Performative Pilgrimage in Search of Malintzin Tenepal." *Text and Performance Quarterly* 25 (2005): 45-58. Print.

Camacho, Amelia. Letter to Yolanda Nava. 24 Nov. 1975. MS. Series I, Box 12, Folder 3. *Comisión Femenil Mexicana Nacional* Archival Collection. CEMA 30. UC Santa Barbara California Ethnic and Multicultural Archives Special Collections, Davidson Library, Santa Barbara, CA.

Castañeda, Oscar Rosales. "Timeline: Movimiento from 1960-1985." *Seattle Civil Rights & Labor History Project*. Seattle Civil Rights & Labor History Project, n.d. Web. 1 Feb. 2010.

Castillo, Ana. *So Far From God*. New York City: New York: W. W. Norton & Company, 2005. Print.

Chabram-Dernersesian, Angie. *Chicana/o cultural studies forum: critical and ethnographic practices*. New York: New York University Press, 2007.

Chicana Service Action Center. Mexican/Chicana Women's Survey. 11 Apr 1972. TS. Series V, Box 41, Folder 13. *Comisión Femenil Mexicana Nacional* Archival Collection. CEMA 30. UC Santa Barbara California Ethnic and Multicultural Archives Special Collections, Davidson Library, Santa Barbara, CA.

Comisión Femenil Mexicana Nacional. Board of Directors Meeting 8-18-1979. Tapes 1 2. *Comisión Femenil Mexicana Nacional* Archival Collection. CEMA 30. UC Santa Barbara California Ethnic and Multicultural Archives Special Collections, Davidson Library, Santa Barbara, CA. Audio.

Copy of a Drawing of a Chicana Revolutionary. MS. Series IX, Box 56. *Comisión Femenil Mexicana Nacional*. Archival Collection. CEMA 30. UC Santa Barbara California Ethnic and Multicultural Archives Special Collections, Davidson Library, Santa Barbara, CA.

_____. Copy of an Organizational Chart. TS. Series I, Box 2, Folder 7. *Comisión Femenil Mexicana Nacional*. Archival Collection. CEMA 30. UC Santa Barbara California Ethnic and Multicultural Archives Special Collections, Davidson Library, Santa Barbara, CA.

_____. "The Experience That Was." *CFM Report* 2.4 (July 1973): 1-3. Series I, Box 23, Folder 4. *Comisión Femenil Mexicana Nacional* Archival Collection. CEMA 30. UC Santa Barbara California Ethnic and Multicultural Archives Special Collections, Davidson Library, Santa Barbara, CA. Print.

_____. "Comisión Femenil Retreat 1973." Box 1, Folder 6. *Comisión Femenil de Los Angeles* Archival Collection. CEMA 30. UCLA Chicano Studies Library. Los Angeles, CA. Print.

_____. "Resolution Adopted by the Women's Workshop 10/10/70 Sacramento, California; [A]Proposal for a Comision Femenil Mexicana." TS. Series IV, Box 34, Folder 3. *Comisión Femenil Mexicana Nacional* Archival Collection. CEMA 30. UC Santa Barbara California Ethnic and Multicultural Archives Special Collections, Davidson Library, Santa Barbara, CA.

_____. "Retreat and Questionnaires, July 11, 1984." TS. Series I, Box 5, Folder 17. *Comisión Femenil Mexicana Nacional* Archival Collection. CEMA 30. UC Santa Barbara California Ethnic and Multicultural Archives Special Collections, Davidson Library, Santa Barbara, CA.

Cushman, Ellen. "Gadugi: A Cherokee Perspective of Working within Communities." From "De-centering Dewey: A Dialogue with Ellen Cushman, Juan Guerra, and Steve Parks." *Reflections* 9.3. 7-17.

Driskill, Qwo-Li. *Yelesalehe Hiwayona Dikanohogida Naiwodusv God Taught Me This Song, It Is Beautiful: Cherokee Performance Rhetorics As Decolonization, Healing, and Continuance*. Diss. Michigan State University, 2008. Print.

Enoch, Jessica. "Survival Stories: Feminist Historiographic Approaches to Chicana Rhetorics of Sterilization Abuse." *Rhetoric Society Quarterly* 35.3 (2005): 5-30. Print.

Flores, Francisca. "Chicana Service Action Center." 18 Mar. 1975. TS. Series IX, Box 53, Folder 6. *Comisión Femenil Mexicana Nacional* Archival Collection. CEMA 30. UC Santa Barbara California Ethnic and Multicultural Archives Special Collections, Davidson Library, Santa Barbara, CA.

Fuentes, Christine. "Memo from Past President." 10 Oct. 1980. TS. Series I, Box 4, Folder 5. *Comisión Femenil Mexicana Nacional* Archival Collection. CEMA 30. UC Santa Barbara California Ethnic and Multicultural Archives Special Collections, Davidson Library, Santa Barbara, CA.

García, Alicia. Telephone Interview. 30 April 2009.

García, Alma M. *Chicana Feminist Thought: The Basic Historical Writings*. New York: Routledge,1997. Print.

García, Sonia R. and Marisela Márquez. "The *Comisión Femenil* : La Voz of a Chicana Organization." 36.1 *Atzlán* (Spring 2011): 149-169. Print.

Gaspar de Alba, Alicia. *La Llorona on the Longfellow Bridge: Poetry y Otras Movidas*. Houston, Texas: Arte Público Press, 2003. Print.

Green, David. "Editor's Introduction: The Community Classroom and African American Contributions to Community Literacy: Moving Forward while Looking Back." *Reflections* 11.1 (Fall 2011): 1-14.

Grosfoguel, Ramón, Nelson Maldonado-Torres, and José David Saldívar, eds. *Latin@s in the World System: Struggles in the Twenty-First Century U.S. Empire*. Paradigm Publishers, 2005. Print.

Longauex y Vásquez, Enriqueta. "The Women of La Raza." TS. Series IX, Box 55, Folder 17. *Comisión Femenil Mexicana Nacional* Archival Collection. CEMA 30. UC Santa Barbara California Ethnic and Multicultural Archives Special Collections, Davidson Library, Santa Barbara, CA.

Lorenzo-Wilson. "Comision Feminil Mexicana, Nacional." 10 July 1973. 1-6. Series II Box 3 folder 3. *Comisión Femenil de Los Angeles* Archival Collection. CEMA 30. UCLA C   hicano Studies Library. Los Angeles, CA. Print.

Martín Alcoff, Linda. *Visible Identifies: Race, Gender, and the Self*. Oxford: Oxford University Press, 2006. Print.

Martín-Alcoff, Linda and Satya P. Mohanty. "Reconsidering Identity Politics: An Introduction." *Identity Politics Reconsidered*. Eds. Linda Martín Alcoff et al. New York, NY: Palgrave, 2006. 1-9. Print.

Matsuda, Gema. "La Chicana Organizes: The *Comisión Femenil Mexicana* in Perspective." *Regeneración* 2.4 (1975): 25-27. Series IX, Box 59, Folder 3. *Comisión Femenil Mexicana Nacional* Archival Collection. CEMA 30. UC Santa Barbara California Ethnic and Multicultural Archives Special Collections, Davidson Library, Santa Barbara, CA. Print.

Mignolo, Walter D. "Huntington's Fears: 'Latinidad' in the Horizon of the Modern/Colonial World." *Latin@s in the World System: Struggles in the Twenty-First Century U.S. Empire*. Eds. Ramón Grosfoguel, Nelson Maldonado-Torres, and José David Saldívar. Paradigm Publishers, 2005. 57-71. Print.

Monberg, Terese. "Listening for Legacies, or How I Began to Hear Dorothy Laigo Cordova, the Pinay behind the Podium known as FAHNS." In *Representations: Doing Asian American Rhetoric*. Eds. Luming Moa and Morris Young. Logan, UT: Utah State U.P., 2008. 83-105. Print.

Moraga, Cherríe. *The Last Generation: prose and poetry*. Boston, MA: South End Press, 1993. Print.

_____. "I Have Dreamed of a Bridge." Moraga and Anzaldúa xviii-xix.

_____. Theory in the Flesh." Moraga and Anzaldúa 23.

Moraga, Cherríe and Anzaldúa, Gloria. *This Bridge Called my Back: Writings by Radical Women of Color.* 2rd ed. New York: Kitchen Table Women of Color Press, 1983. Print.

Moya, Paula. *Learning from Experience: Minority Identities, Multicultural Struggles.* University of California Press, 2002. Print.

Pasadena Board of *Comisión Femenil Mexicana.* Memo to Gloria Moreno-Wycoff. 16 Oct. 1980. TS. Series I, Box 4, Folder 5. *Comisión Femenil Mexicana Nacional Archival Collection.* CEMA 30. UC Santa Barbara California Ethnic and Multicultural Archives Special Collections, Davidson Library, Santa Barbara, CA.

Pérez, Emma. *The Decolonial Imaginary: writing Chicanas into history.* Bloomington & Indianapolis, IN, USA: Indiana U.P., 1999. Print.

Ramirez-Dhoore, Dora Alicia. "The Cyberborderland: Searching the Web for Xicanidad." *Chicana/Latina Studies: The Journal of Mujeres Activas en Letras y Cambio Social.* 5.1 (Fall 2005): 12-47. Print.

Kendall Leon is an Assistant Professor of Rhetoric and Composition at Purdue University. Her research interests include cultural rhetorics, research methodology, digital writing and community engagement.

Becoming Qualified to Teach Low-literate Refugees: A Case Study of One Volunteer Instructor

Kristen H. Perry

This case study investigates Carolyn, an effective volunteer ESL and literacy instructor of adult African refugees, in order to understand both what it means to be a qualified instructor, and also how community-based volunteer instructors may become more qualified. The study's findings suggest that Carolyn's qualifications are a combination of personal dispositions, such as cultural sensitivity, and professional behaviors, including self-education, seeking mentoring and outside expertise, and purposeful reflection on her teaching. Several implications for supporting community-based volunteer literacy and ESL instructors emerge from these findings.

English language learners (ELLs) represent the fastest-growing sector of adult education in the U.S., and refugees represent an increasingly important segment of this population (Bricket et al. 1; Kerwin 2). In 2007, approximately 48,000 refugees resettled in the U.S.; this number increased to sixty thousand in 2008, and the resettlement ceiling has been raised to eighty thousand for 2011 (Kerwin 3-4). The U.S. also has accepted refugees from an increasingly diverse range of nations. In 2009, for example, refugees from over sixty countries resettled in the U.S. – twenty-three of which were African nations (Kerwin 6). Another important trend is that refugees are increasingly being resettled in cities that are non-traditional gateways for immigrants, such as Lansing, Michigan, and Omaha, Nebraska. The government's Preferred Communities program purposefully resettles refugees in small and mid-size communities "beyond the main urban centers in which those newly arrived have traditionally concentrated" (USCRI), based on a belief that these communities are better prepared to meet newcomers' needs. Lexington, Kentucky represents one of the communities in which increasing numbers of refugees have settled. Caseworkers at the local refugee resettlement agency, for example, reported that over 150 individuals and families resettled in Lexington in 2008 alone; this number jumped to 230 in 2009 and exceeded three hundred for 2010.

Educational opportunities, particularly in English as a Second Language (ESL) and Adult Basic Literacy (ABL), are crucial for refugees to obtain jobs and become self-sufficient. Adult refugees come to language and literacy programs with a wide variety of prior educational experiences, yet they often have challenges and needs that differ from those of other adult learners (Anderson et al. 15-18; Barton et al. 102-103; Perry 35; Muth & Perry). For example, Barton et al. found that refugees have higher levels of confidence in educational settings than other adult learners and often already are very highly educated (102-103). However, other refugees are unschooled or had severely interrupted schooling (Anderson et al. 15-18).

Unfortunately, those who tutor or teach in ESL and ABL programs often are not well equipped to deal with the specific needs of adult refugees (Suda 22). ESL/ABL classes and individual tutoring frequently are staffed by community volunteers who tend to have limited – if any – training or experience in teaching ESL or literacy (Ceprano 63; Chisman 3-4; McKenna and Fitzpatrick 40; Ziegler, McCallum, and Bell 131). Although some universities offer certification programs, few instructors take advantage of the programs (Chisman 3-4), which may not be especially surprising when we consider that a large percentage of the potential clientele are unpaid instructors who volunteer their time. This lack of training and expertise among adult literacy and adult ESL instructors is problematic, as these educators are expected, but unprepared, to work with students whose learning needs may be significant. While volunteer instructors bring interest, commitment, and passion (Belzer 560) to their teaching, some adult literacy and ESL programs experience high rates of volunteer instructor turnover (Perry 78), which may be due in part to frustration and feelings of unpreparedness.

Recent attention has been paid to issues of credentialing and certification among the adult education teaching force (e.g., Chisman), although this attention is focused primarily on paid instructors and not volunteers. Despite the fact that adult ESL instruction faces many challenges and problems related to training, certification, or credentialing among instructors and tutors, and despite the fact that requirements for training, certification, and credentialing typically do not apply to volunteer instructors, there nevertheless are success stories that can offer important lessons. Chisman calls for studies "to investigate the characteristics of teachers who do and do not participate in [credentialing] systems, and why or why not, and to ask how they think the systems might be improved" (26). This case study is, in part, a response to that call.

In this manuscript, I present the case of Carolyn, an experienced but uncredentialed instructor of a low-literate ESL class for adult African refugees in Kentucky, in order to explore issues related to teaching qualifications among volunteer adult literacy/ESL educators. Carolyn had little formal training to teach, yet her teaching practices and her prior experiences suggested that while she may not be *certified* to teach, she may, in fact, be very *qualified* to do so. The following research questions shaped this analysis: What does it mean to be *qualified* to teach pre- or low-literate English language learners? How might uncredentialed or non-certified instructors become qualified?

Certification Versus Qualification

As Chisman notes in *Closing the Gap: The Challenge of Certification and Credentialing in Adult Education,* "teacher certification and credentialing are orphan issues in adult education" (11). Adult ESL and adult ABL programs often are run on shoestring budgets by community organizations using volunteer educators who may have little – if any – professional experience or training in language acquisition theories, effective methods for teaching language and literacy, or other pedagogical content knowledge

(Anderson et al. 47; Chisman, *iii*; McKenna and Fitzpatrick 40). Chisman concludes that most adult educators are "'experienced but not expert', for two basic reasons: few have had extensive formal training in adult basic skills instruction and too few suitable in-service programs are available to them" (*iii*). This lack of training may result in poor quality instruction and poor student outcomes. For example, in a case study of volunteer adult literacy tutors, Ceprano finds that participants typically utilized teaching strategies based on what they were exposed to as learners, rather than those grounded in current theory and practice, which "could ultimately lead to feelings of frustration and defeat for their clients" (63).

In addition to being "orphaned" in adult education policy and practice, the issue of adult educator credentialing, particularly concerning volunteer educators, also has received limited attention in educational research. Of course, the lack of preparation for volunteer tutors in adult literacy has been known for some time (e.g., Crandall 2). Although recent research has attended to the issue of instructor qualifications in adult literacy (e.g., Belzer; Chisman), research investigating issues of volunteer teacher credentialing in adult ESL, particularly for instructors who also work with clients who are developing basic literacy skills, is scant.

Another challenge is that the terminology used to refer to these issues is contested. Chisman (5) notes that "the terms used to describe the process of establishing standards and measuring whether teachers meet them often carry symbolic and bureaucratic 'baggage' both within and outside the field." These contested terms include *certification, credentialing, endorsement,* and *professionalization*. According to Chisman, *credentialing* may be viewed as relatively neutral and signifies "the process of measuring proficiency by any means or for any purpose" (6). In contrast to *certification*, which implies earning a certificate or some other endorsement from an accredited entity, such as a university, *credentialing* implies flexibility in evaluating teaching proficiency. Yet the flexibility of *credentialing* is also problematic, because credentialing in adult education may mean holding a teaching certificate, but it also may mean having a bachelor's degree in any field (Ziegler, McCallum, and Bell 131). Thus, someone with a BA in art history or a BS in biology is credentialed and, thus, supposedly qualified to teach basic education or literacy to adults.

Of course, the term *qualified* itself is also contested, as a result of legislation like No Child Left Behind that requires all certified teachers to be "highly qualified," which usually means that teachers can pass a standardized test (Berry 2). However, as Berry points out, such a definition is, at best, limited: teachers may be able to pass a test, but they may not be effective in the classroom. Instead, Berry suggests that highly-qualified teachers "are teachers who know not only their subject matter, but also how to organize and teach their lessons in ways that assure diverse students can learn those subjects....Highly qualified teachers don't just teach well-designed, standards-based lessons: They know how and why their students learn" (2). Following Berry and Chisman, in this paper, I distinguish between *certified teachers*, who may hold particular certifications or endorsements, and *qualified teachers* who may not necessarily possess these documents, but who demonstrate both knowledge and skill related to teaching and the ability to help their students learn. That is, a qualified teacher may or may not be certified and vice versa.

Adult Literacy and ESL Instructor Preparation

The education field has long accepted that teachers need several types of knowledge, including content knowledge, knowledge of teaching theory and practice, and pedagogical content knowledge, or "ways of representing and formulating the subject that make it comprehensible to others" (Shulman 9). In addition to the typical types of instructor knowledge related to issues such as learner-centered instruction techniques, building learning communities, and appropriate assessments, Chisman suggests that those who instruct in basic literacy, GED, and life skills ESL programs require additional expertise, such as "managing open-entry classrooms with students of different abilities" (2).

Ziegler, McCallum, and Bell (also Bell, Ziegler, and McCallum) investigated (a) volunteer educators' training and certification and (b) their pedagogical content knowledge with respect to teaching adult literacy. Participants' self-assessment of their knowledge "rarely corresponded to their actual mastery of that content" (Bell, Ziegler, and McCallum 555) or assessment of what they needed to learn. These researchers also found that credentialing (defined as either a bachelor's or higher degree, or a teaching certificate) mattered, in that credentialed instructors knew significantly more than uncredentialed instructors (Ziegler, McCallum, and Bell 136). Volunteers had about the same level of knowledge as paid educators, but unlike paid instructors, volunteers spent most of their professional development in independent study, as opposed to in conferences, workshops, or college courses.

Chisman's report notes that "numerous barriers prevent teachers from increasing their knowledge and skills, meeting standards, and earning credentials" (*iii*), and this may be particularly true for instructors who are unpaid, community-based volunteers. However, research also suggests that, even when volunteer instructors do have access to training programs, those programs may be ineffective. Ceprano (63) found that tutors' instructional practices bore little resemblance to the techniques they learned in training, instead reflecting their own learning experiences. Training may have limited effectiveness in part because it is so short; volunteers typically receive fifteen to twenty hours—if any—of training (Crandall 2). Such training can convey broad ideas but is less likely to convey technical aspects of teaching literacy (Belzer 135).

Methodology

Few studies have examined preparation to teach adult literacy (Ziegler, McCallum, and Bell 132); this is especially true with respect to teaching adult ESL, particularly to students with limited literacy skills. This case study offers an analysis of Carolyn, a community-based, volunteer adult ESL and literacy instructor, with a focus on her non-traditional qualifications to teach.

Research Context

Lexington, Kentucky is one of many communities that has seen an exponential growth in refugee populations, due to the Preferred Communities resettlement program (USCRI). Several organizations offer free ESL and/or ABL instruction to adult refugees, including the local community college, various community organizations, and some local churches (details of these programs can be found in Perry and Hart). Carolyn's class began after she was approached by both the refugee resettlement agency and a community-based literacy center; they were in desperate need of a class for a group of older African adults, all of whom needed to learn to read and write for the first time, in addition to learning English. Carolyn's class met at the community-based literacy center in the heart of downtown; this center offered or supported a variety of literacy-oriented programs, such as after-school tutoring programs, adult ESL, French and Spanish language classes, and workshops for aspiring writers. Carolyn's class met one morning a week in a small library room that featured resources for writers.

Carolyn's group consisted of three to four adult refugees, all in their 60s or older, who originally came from either the Democratic Republic of Congo (DRC) or Burundi. As Carolyn wrote on her questionnaire, "My class may be somewhat unique in that the students are older, their goals being perhaps different. They enjoy the comfortable setting, the opportunity to visit with each other, and the chance to learn some English." Carolyn indicated that, due to the nature of her students, this class was very different than previous adult ESL classes she had taught, in which her students had attained high levels of prior formal education. In contrast, Carolyn's current students had no formal schooling, and this impacted her teaching in many ways. As she noted,

> I was amazed, one time I had them cut out objects, that they didn't know how to use scissors. You know, they just had not done that. We learn that from the time that we're children. And holding a pencil, forming those letters, and I'm still [teaching] that.

Carolyn

I first met Carolyn when the local refugee resettlement agency asked us to help put on a training session for new volunteer tutors. This training session offered a brief orientation to working with refugees and teaching English. Carolyn brought several bags full of teaching materials – most of which she had created herself – that she used with her adult ESL and literacy students. Knowing little else about her, I assumed that Carolyn was a veteran, certified teacher. I learned that, while Carolyn indeed had taught literacy and ESL classes for many years and also was a retired school librarian, she was not a certified teacher. Nevertheless, the quality of the materials she created, her own descriptions of her teaching, and the glowing recommendations from caseworkers and others familiar with her teaching, suggested that Carolyn might be an effective teacher of low-literate adult refugees. In the following sections, I provide a fuller description of Carolyn and her teaching.

I recruited Carolyn to be part of a larger study of educational opportunities for refugees in Lexington (e.g. Perry and Hart; Perry and Mallozzi). Carolyn completed an open-ended questionnaire and also agreed to participate in a follow-up interview and to allow observations in her classroom.

Data Collection Methods

Data sources for this case study included Carolyn's responses to the open-ended questionnaire and semi-structured interview, along with observations of her teaching. Among other topics, the questionnaire included items with respect to Carolyn's training and relevant experiences. The semi-structured interview gathered more in-depth data regarding her preparation for and experiences with teaching refugees. An undergraduate research assistant participated in this interview, and we audio-recorded and transcribed the interview verbatim. We shared the transcript with Carolyn in order to (a) check for accuracy, (b) clarify any points, and (c) offer an opportunity to omit any sensitive data.

The research assistant and I also conducted two open-ended observations in Carolyn's class. Observations focused on instructional techniques and Carolyn's interactions with her students. We wrote field notes, to which we added more detail after the observation; we immediately shared the field notes with Carolyn in order to check for accuracy and to identify sensitive data.

Data Analysis

Analysis was ongoing both during and after data collection. The first stage involved coding Carolyn's questionnaire, looking for broad themes and then developing specific codes for activities, beliefs, and needs. Differences in coding were resolved through discussion. Analysis of the questionnaire also guided some questions we asked during the interview. Analysis of the interview transcript proceeded in the same manner. Throughout analysis, we wrote analytic research memos to raise questions about initial data or to explain and interpret findings (Emerson, Fretz, and Shaw 155-162). We validated our research findings through triangulation and member-checking. In addition to viewing and commenting on transcripts and field notes, Carolyn also reviewed an early version of this manuscript.

Carolyn: Snapshot of a Volunteer Instructor

Carolyn was an effective instructor of adult refugees who were simultaneously learning English and learning to read and write. She was trained and certified as a school librarian, and she had many years of experience working as a librarian in international schools. Additionally, she had ten years of experience teaching ESL to adults. Following her retirement and return to the U.S., Carolyn began teaching ESL at the local literacy center, working with people who were "well educated in their own language," including native Spanish speakers and graduate students from China and Japan. She contrasted this prior experience with her current situation in teaching unschooled African adults:

> If they were literate in their own language, there's enough similarity that you can build on that all the time, and you could talk about what a noun and verb are, so it's quite different. And because [my current students] speak so little, it's very difficult to even explain things to them. That's why I use so many hands-on things and so many pictures and objects, because we don't have a lot of ways to communicate.

Despite her many years of experience working as a librarian in international schools, her participation in the literacy center's training program, and her years of experience teaching ESL with adults, Carolyn indicated that she did not necessarily feel prepared to teach her students. Carolyn's unease seemed to stem in large part from the nature of the students she was now teaching – students whose English learning also involved learning to read and write for the first time. As Carolyn explained,

> I'm not trained as a reading teacher, you know. I'm trained as a librarian, and I taught – I was a teacher in a sense in that I taught kids how to use the library, but I'm not a reading teacher. So, I'm not always sure that I know sequentially how to go about teaching somebody to read.

Analyzing Carolyn's response in relation to her training and experience suggests that being qualified to teach is a complex matter. Although Carolyn had a number of years of experience in the field of education and had taught adult ELLs for a decade, teaching low-literate adult ELLs felt entirely different to her. Her feelings were common among community-based instructors in Lexington, who indicated the same general feeling of unpreparedness for the teaching they were being asked to do with adult refugees, no matter their level of training, certification, or amount of prior teaching experience (Perry and Hart).

Carolyn explained that "the only training I have is the training that they [the literacy center] gave me, which was, I don't know, 12 hours or something." I asked Carolyn to evaluate whether or not this was enough training to do what the literacy organization and the refugee resettlement agency hoped she could do with her particular learners. She responded,

> Sometimes, I do question that. You know, I've gotten to a point where I'm not sure I can take them to the next step very well. I don't have anybody telling me what the next step should be. … Every week I'm figuring out for myself what's the best thing for me to do for them. And, you know, I've gotten them to the point where they can read a little bit, but I don't know that I'll ever get very—well, for one thing as you know I only see them one hour a week. You're not going to get a whole lot of progress.

Carolyn's response to my question revealed a great deal about her level of preparedness, about herself as an instructor, and about the context in which she was being asked to teach. First, her response suggested a great deal of uncertainty about her teaching; not only was she "not sure" she could take her students to the next level, but she also was unsure even of what that next level might be. Her response indicated a sense of isolation, in addition to the uncertainty, as she noted that she had to figure out "for myself what's the best thing." Yet, her response also suggested a pragmatic awareness of the limitations placed on her teaching by the context – even a credentialed, highly-experienced literacy teacher likely would not see much progress in students who only received one hour of literacy and language instruction per week.

Being a Qualified Instructor

Although she was not *certified* to teach English or literacy, and despite the fact that she felt unprepared for the task of teaching ESL to low-literate adults, Carolyn exhibited many characteristics of teaching professionalism that might contribute to being *qualified* to teach. These characteristics fell into three themes: (1) Carolyn's *cross-cultural awareness and sensitivity*, (2) the fact that she was a *reflective practitioner,* and (3) her *philosophy of teaching and learning*. These themes suggest routes that other instructors in similar circumstances might follow in order to enhance their own professionalism and qualifications.

Cross-Cultural Awareness and Sensitivity

Carolyn's cross-cultural awareness and sensitivity to her students grew out of her personal background and professional experiences. Carolyn and her husband both had significant experience abroad, having worked in international schools in a variety of Middle Eastern countries. As Carolyn explained,

> We started out in Kuwait and spent two years at the American School of Kuwait. Then, we went to Saudi Arabia and spent six years there, and then to the United Arab Emirates and lived in the emirate of Abu Dhabi and worked at the American School there for 12 years.

Extensive experience with living overseas and working in international schools seemed to foster a high level of cultural awareness in Carolyn that served her students well. Carolyn herself believed "that having worked with children from lots of different cultures has made me more perceptive." She shared a vignette from her previous ESL teaching experience, in which she was able to directly draw upon her international experiences:

> I think it's just been wonderful that I've had the opportunity to work with kids from all different countries, and for instance, for a little while I had a student from somewhere in Arabia, I can't even think where it was. But the first time she came in, I greeted her in Arabic…and you would have thought that I had given her a platter of food or something.

Carolyn's cross-cultural awareness translated into a sensitivity toward her students and an understanding of the many challenges facing them. This understanding and sensitivity, in turn, including understanding what it was like to be an outsider unable to speak the language, likely influenced her teaching and her relationships with her students. Indeed, this kind of cross-cultural sensitivity is a disposition that teacher preparation programs often seek in prospective teachers.

Being a Reflective Practitioner

Throughout her interview, Carolyn demonstrated that she reflected a great deal on her experiences and her teaching practice. This reflection – a disposition endorsed in teacher-training programs – served Carolyn well; being a reflective practitioner in many ways helped her overcome her feeling of being unqualified to teach. Carolyn clearly did not feel prepared to teach adult literacy, yet she also believed that her prior experiences had helped to prepare her for this teaching, at least in part: "I think having an education background is really helpful … I had worked with kids for so long that I was not afraid at all to just jump in and try things." Indeed, in contrast to her earlier statement of uncertainty about teaching African refugee adults to read, Carolyn described a success story with one of her students, Eugenie (all students' names are pseudonyms), with whom she had been working one-on-one for some time:

> I had gotten to the point where I had made a little book for her and photographs with a picture with the two of us. "Eugenie is short, Carolyn is tall. Eugenie and Carolyn are friends" you know. I was adding to this little booklet, and then I started getting a couple of other people. All of a sudden I had to pull back from that, because I had to go back to the beginning. But I honestly think that if I could just work with her, she'd be reading now, really reading, because she is so bright. And yet, I'm sure she never learned to read or write her own language.

Carolyn's success with Eugenie suggests that, while she may not have felt confident in her abilities to teach both English and literacy to adult refugees, she nevertheless was a successful instructor who was able to think carefully about her students' abilities and learning needs.

In fact, Carolyn reported engaging in routine, purposeful reflection on her own instruction and her students' learning as a regular part of her teaching practice:

> I spent 20 years as a librarian; I tend to be a very organized person, and most of the time when I come home from a class, if I have time, I sit down right then. I make note of what we did, what worked, what didn't work, and notes about what I want to do next week. And then I always type up a lesson plan.

Carolyn attributed this routine reflection to her experience as a librarian, which suggests that prior experiences *outside* the field of education may be beneficial for volunteer instructors. Carolyn, for example, was able to draw upon professional habits related to organization and research skills to analyze her learners' strengths and needs, and to educate herself about learning and teaching. As with cultural awareness and sensitivity, Carolyn's habit of purposefully reflecting on what did – or did not – work in her individual lessons is one that teacher education programs attempt to cultivate in prospective teachers. Strong teachers constantly reflect on their teaching and their students' learning, and Carolyn clearly exemplified this disposition.

Philosophy of Teaching & Learning
Taking note of what worked (or did not work) appeared to have helped Carolyn to develop a philosophy of teaching and learning for low-literate adult ELLs. Evidence of Carolyn's philosophy occurred in statements of belief, such as when she explained, "I believe that repetition is just essential." Or, as I noted in field notes during a pause in her class,

> Even though she focuses on the sounds, she also thinks sight words are important. Carolyn said that she learned to read before phonics, and

that she had used sight words to learn to read herself. She believes sight words are important particularly because students who have always learned by listening need to focus on what things look like.

Carolyn's many descriptions of her own teaching, along with my observations, demonstrated that she engaged in many effective pedagogical techniques for teaching beginning literacy, as I will describe. Carolyn's belief in "just jumping in and trying things," coupled with her disposition as a reflective practitioner, likely worked in concert to help her become an effective teacher. Her willingness to experiment with new techniques, and her regular reflection on what did and did not work, suggest that prior experience and specific habits might contribute to being qualified to teach, even when teachers have limited training.

During our interview, Carolyn described how she structured the beginning of her lessons – a technique she had adapted from her own language learning when she took a Spanish language class:

> I start every class with what day is today. And I found a couple years ago, when I took a Spanish class at the [literacy] center, that it was comforting to me if the class began with something I knew. So, even though we do it every single time, it's a way to begin, and everybody knows the answer. So, everybody feels good about being able to answer the question, and I have one student who has been with me the longest, who is VERY bright. I always ask her first, so that the other students can model her, and so we always start with what day is today and what is the date? What is the year? What is the season? And what is the weather? And then I write it down and my star student is at the point now, where once I have that all written out on the white board, she can read it all. And she'll come up, point to the words and read the sentences, and then each of the other students will come up.

Observations of Carolyn's teaching confirmed that her lessons always started off in this manner, including the routines of stating the date and the season and describing the day's weather – a beginning literacy routine very similar to the calendar routines found in many U.S. primary grade classrooms. The observed lessons then followed a common structure that involved reviewing something the students had recently learned (e.g., months of the year, words that begin with a specific sound), introducing a new phonics concept (e.g., the letter of the day, rhyming words), and writing practice related to the phonics concept (e.g., words that start with the letter of the day or that rhyme). If time remained in the lesson, Carolyn sometimes had her students read from homemade pattern books with predictable text (e.g., "I see ____."). Carolyn purposefully structured her lessons in this way, in accordance with a philosophy of learning she had developed through her prior teaching experience:

> I believe that repetition is just essential, and you know I've worked with enough kids, like I mentioned earlier, I always go with my best student first. Nobody seems to mind that, because I'm almost certain she'll know

the answer, and then I go to the one, the next one, you know, from the top and let them go. By the time I get to the last person, they've heard the answer three times, and that gives them an opportunity to be successful. And I think that comes from experience. Just, maybe, it's a very small thing to realize that repetition and the need to feel successful when you're learning.

Like many effective literacy teachers, Carolyn used visual aids, hands-on materials, and realia in her teaching to support her students' language and literacy learning. Although she purchased some materials from a local teacher supply store, she created most materials herself in order to make them appropriate to adult students and to connect them with her students' lives and needs. During one lesson, for example, Carolyn reviewed vegetable vocabulary the students had learned in previous lessons, using her homemade cards. The cards had words typed in a large font, illustrated with colorful clip-art illustrations, mounted on green construction paper (Carolyn always mounted words from a given theme on the same color of paper):

> Carolyn holds up the cards, and the students say the vegetables. For many of the veggies (e.g., cabbage, carrots, broccoli, and garlic), Carolyn asks the students if they have it in Africa. The students lean forward to look at the cards. Carolyn then picks up the carrot card and asks, "What color are the carrots?" She does this for several veggies. The students debate whether the beans are red or brown (they are brown). The students typically reply with one word answers (e.g., "red," "orange," or "green"). Then, Carolyn repeats their answer in a complete sentence: "The broccoli is green." Carolyn asks Valérie to give her the pumpkin. She asks Eugenie to give her the carrots. She asks Boniface to give her the tomatoes. The students locate the appropriate veggie cards and hand them to Carolyn. Carolyn repeats this with the remaining veggies, asking each student in turn. When Boniface gets stuck on *cucumber*, Eugenie whispers something to him.

This excerpt from Carolyn's teaching typified her instructional style and was evidence of her teaching & learning philosophy in action. Carolyn used a variety of effective scaffolding techniques for developing both language and literacy, such as using picture cards with word labels, repeating predictable questions, allowing students to answer with one-word responses, modeling appropriate grammatical structures, and encouraging peer support. Additionally, asking students if the depicted vegetables were available in Africa scaffolded students' learning by drawing on their prior knowledge and encouraging them to make personal connections to the concept being taught.

As in the field note excerpt, Carolyn's teaching frequently relied on realia and homemade materials that she used to teach vocabulary, phonics, or other literacy concepts. According to Carolyn, this was a technique she had learned after consulting with her sister-in-law, "who taught Montessori for years." As Carolyn explained,

Her suggestion was to teach the sounds of the letters rather than the names of the letters, and that may be what kindergarten teachers do, I don't know, to take very different sounds. So I took the word *bat* first, and taught B and A and T and slowly produced the letter sounds and words that would go with the letters. When I was teaching B, I took a basket and walked around my house and gathered up anything that began with a B, and I'd do the same thing for other letters of the alphabet.

Indeed, Carolyn started using realia during her very first day of teaching language and literacy to this group of students. She reflected:

I remember the first class was in February, and it was really cold, so I grabbed every color of jacket I had, you know, red, blue, green, pink, and sweaters, and mittens and gloves, and hats, I think, which was a lot. And so I started out with the names of each of those, the colors, and how many there were. And that was just the beginning, you know, so then I kind of got the idea to use themes.

Using this type of realia was so integral to Carolyn's teaching that she kept a permanent bag of materials and brought it to every class. I initially had seen Carolyn's bag of teaching materials when I first met her at the workshop we conducted for other volunteers, and I was able to get a closer look at it during one of my observations of her teaching. Carolyn's bag included many objects she had gathered or purchased for teaching, including colored pencils, balloons, buttons, and pens, all of which she used for counting, colors, and object names. She had a bag of coins and a few small bills for counting money, along with small clocks for telling time. Her bag included word cards and other flashcards – some store-bought, but mostly homemade. Her store-bought flashcards indicated vowels, consonants, and pictures with word labels. Homemade cards covered themed topics such as items in the living room, bedroom, bathroom, and kitchen. She also created sets of homemade cards of everyday words that started with specific letters, such as H (e.g., hat, hanger, hammer, husband), which she used when she was teaching letters and letter-sound correspondences. Carolyn's bag also included a file box that contained many pictures of items or concepts, such as clothing, rooms in a house, or seasons, which were "just pictures I collected out of catalogues and magazines." Carolyn showed me sets of color strips made of tagboard that she gives to students when they come to her class for the first time. She explained that she always carries this bag of materials "because you never know who's going to be here" and because she sometimes found herself with extra time at the end of her lesson for review: "If I have five minutes at the end, I'll pull it out and we'll just go back and practice."

The portrait I have painted of Carolyn's teaching shows that, while she was not certified in either ESL or literacy education, her teaching was grounded in pedagogical practices that are known to be effective in teaching language and literacy. Carolyn's descriptions of and reflections on her own teaching suggest that she took a great deal of care in thinking about her learners, in thinking about their prior experiences and learning needs, and in preparing lessons that fit her learners.

Becoming a Qualified Instructor: Implications

Carolyn's case suggests that, for volunteer teachers of adult refugees, being qualified may involve a mixture of experiences and professional habits that can be cultivated over time. For example, unlike some volunteer tutors, Carolyn had a great deal of experience in both educational and cross-cultural settings, and she was able to draw upon these experiences to inform her own teaching. Her professional experiences as a librarian also likely disposed her toward helpful habits such as being organized and prepared and also knowing how to seek information through research. Indeed, another important theme among the findings of this study was that much of Carolyn's qualification to teach was due to the efforts she made at professional self-education. In addition to purposefully reflecting on her teaching, Carolyn engaged in behaviors designed to increase her professional knowledge.

Because Carolyn did not have any specific training to teach literacy, and because she felt unprepared to teach adult students who needed to read and write, she actively sought information and taught herself the knowledge needed to educate her learners. Part of this self-education process involved seeking guidance and mentoring from experts. When she was approached "to take on a pre-literate group," Carolyn's initial reaction was "I don't know how to do this ... I don't know where to begin." Instead of turning down the opportunity, Carolyn sought expertise from her sister-in-law, who was a Montessori teacher, and from an experienced adult ESL teacher:

> I actually got in touch with [someone] who teaches at [the community college] ... I emailed her and said what do you think? And she emailed back and said, "You can do this, you're a librarian—go on the Internet and do some research!" [*laughs*] ... So that's what I did, and I was amazed really at what I found.

The Challenge of Credentialing Requirements for Volunteers

Finding and retaining qualified instructors is a great challenge for adult education in general (Chisman *iii*); this challenge is even greater for community-based programs that are staffed by volunteer instructors and tutors, as are many adult ESL programs. Calls have been made (e.g., Chisman) to increase the qualifications of the adult education teaching force, to increase the knowledge and skills that instructors possess, and to ensure that they are credentialed. While these goals are important, they are less feasible for volunteer instructors in community-based programs than they are for instructors who are paid, whether part-time or full-time. In fact, formal credentialing was one technique that was surprisingly unsuccessful for Carolyn; shortly after she first began teaching ESL ten years prior to the study, Carolyn had enrolled in education courses at a local university. However, she quickly discovered that the available programs and courses did not fit her perceived needs:

> After I'd been back [in the U.S.] and I was doing this about a year, I thought, "Well, maybe I should just, you know, take some coursework," and I started a class at UK, but I had to take this semester of theory class ... first, and I got into the class and I thought, you know, I'm in my 50s,

and I've been teaching for 20 years. I'm not going to sit for a semester through this theory class. This was not what I want, and this is not what I need, and so I dropped the class, because I wanted some nitty-gritty, what to do in the classroom kind of class, and I would suspect that most people like me would feel that way. I did not need another graduate-level class in theory.

Carolyn's narrative illustrates a number of potentially significant issues. Importantly, her narrative suggests that some volunteer instructors, particularly those who make it past a few months of teaching, may be willing to pursue – and pay for – university coursework related to language and literacy pedagogy, even if they are "just" unpaid community-based volunteers. However, Carolyn's experience also reveals some of the barriers toward this type of professional development. For example, requiring theory classes as prerequisites may deter those instructors who are already in the field and looking for immediate solutions to the challenges they are facing with their current students. While theory certainly is relevant for all instructors, other methods and models – such as embedding theory into other pedagogical content instruction – may be far more effective with these instructors, who may seek to enhance their qualifications without undergoing an entire certification program.

Supporting Volunteer Professional Development
Community-based ESL and literacy programs certainly can work toward recruiting instructors and tutors who are qualified and credentialed, although this may not be a realistic or pragmatic goal for most programs, if they must rely on the generosity and free time of volunteers. Instead of requiring certification or other credentialing for volunteer instructors in community-based adult ESL and adult literacy programs, it may make more sense to support these instructors in specific ways that will help them work toward being qualified.

Ongoing professional development.
Directors and staff of community-based adult education programs can work in conjunction with education departments at local colleges and universities, or with local school districts, to offer periodic professional development workshops to volunteer instructors. Experts at local colleges, universities, or school districts also can develop free or low-cost online modules that are targeted to volunteer instructors in community-based programs. Online modules could be credit-bearing with a local institution, or they could offer some sort of certificate of completion. Some online modules could be standard, offering training and professional development on general topics related to adult language and literacy pedagogy, while others could be developed specific to the local contexts in which volunteers are teaching. For example, for instructors such as Carolyn, who face a large population of African refugees who have never been to school, a module could be developed that helps instructors understand differences in teaching adult literacy with unschooled adults versus teaching adult literacy with schooled adults who have reading disabilities. Online modules might avoid the pitfall Carolyn faced when she attempted to enroll in a local university program, but found

she would need to take theory courses before she was able to take courses that would have better addressed her immediate needs.

Professional connections.
Carolyn's case illustrates the importance of volunteer instructors having access to peer mentors, such as the instructor at the community college and her Montessori-teaching sister-in-law. Community-based education programs can foster formal mentoring partnerships – matching a mentor with an apprentice instructor, providing access to a local expert at a university or school district – or individual instructors can seek out such partnerships on their own. Other types of partnership opportunities, such as online social networking sites in which instructors can connect with each other or with experts, can serve as additional ways in which instructors might increase their professional qualifications, as they share knowledge and resources. For example, instructors and experts might set up professional reading book clubs – either online or face-to-face – in which they have opportunities to increase their knowledge of learning and teaching. Finally, as Carolyn's case suggested, having access to appropriate literacy teaching materials for adults was a great challenge; as a result, Carolyn invested a great deal of time, money, and energy in developing and making her own teaching materials. Community-based programs might offer workshops, similar to scrapbooking parties or quilting bees, in which instructors gather together to create teaching materials that they could keep themselves or contribute to a common materials library. Alternately, instructors could organize such materials-making parties themselves.

Encouraging self-education.
The amount of time and energy that Carolyn put into educating herself about effective language and literacy instruction suggests that self-education is an important technique for volunteer instructors of adult ESL and adult literacy, particularly those who may feel that they are unprepared and/or have little in the way of support. Finding ways to support individual volunteer instructors' self-education, whether through professional development modules, social networking opportunities, or individual reading and research, is important. Additionally, Carolyn's case suggests that purposeful reflection may be critical for volunteer instructors as an important way to increase their teaching qualifications. Helping these instructors understand that reflecting on their own teaching – or even giving them a brief introduction to action research in educational settings – may be an effective way to increase the qualifications of instructors who are not certified to teach, and who are not compensated for the important teaching they do.

Conclusion: Being (And Becoming) Qualified

Volunteer instructors in community-based programs, like Carolyn, are in great need of opportunities to increase their qualifications to teach (Chisman *iii*); however, this need also exists for paid instructors and for instructors who already have some credentialing or certification, particularly if their credentials do not fit the population they are teaching. As the case of Carolyn suggests, *being qualified* is more than a matter of holding a specific certification (e.g., in literacy education or in ESL education). Being qualified includes having content knowledge, pedagogical knowledge, and pedagogical-content knowledge related to teaching language and literacy to adults (Shulman 9), but these areas of knowledge are not sufficient. In addition to holding certain types of knowledge, being qualified also may mean having had certain experiences and specific dispositions that can support a teacher in her efforts to work with adult ELLs.

As Carolyn's case demonstrates, prior experiences can contribute to being qualified to teach. Many volunteers may come to adult ESL and adult literacy programs with prior experiences in education (Perry). However, prior experiences in education may not necessarily prepare instructors to work with adults or or for the specifics of teaching language and/or literacy. Educators trained for the elementary field, for example, may not be adequately prepared to meet the unique learning needs of adults. Similarly, secondary educators trained in fields like math and science education may not have the knowledge or skills necessary to teach language and/or literacy. As a result, even credentialed teachers may need opportunities to increase their qualifications with respect to working with adult learners, teaching ESL, teaching literacy, or any combination of the three. While requiring adult educators to complete coursework or enroll in continuing education may be feasible for part-time or full-time paid instructors, requiring credentialing or formal coursework is unrealistic in volunteer-taught, community-based adult literacy and ESL programs. However, increasing volunteer instructors' qualifications through other avenues is both possible and promising.

Carolyn's case illustrates some ways in which community-based programs may support instructors' development of qualifications, or in which individual instructors may seek to enhance their own qualifications. Yet, Carolyn's case does not provide the whole story; it raises questions for future research. For example, if cross-cultural awareness is important, how can this quality be fostered in instructors, or potential instructors, who have had limited experience with people who are culturally different from themselves? If dispositions and experiences, regardless of whether those experiences involve teaching, are important, how can adult education programs effectively recruit and/or screen for instructors with those qualities? How can programs foster purposeful reflection and the development of appropriate philosophies of teaching and learning among volunteer instructors? In short, the value of this case study of Carolyn and her effective teaching is that it offers both a portrait of what a qualified—although uncredentialed—teacher may look like and some hints toward supporting the development of these qualifications in other teachers. Yet, such a case study cannot offer conclusive answers about increasing the qualifications of volunteer instructors; much further research is required.

Works Cited

Anderson, Jim, et al. *Implementing an Intergenerational Literacy Program with Authentic Literacy Instruction: Challenges, Responses, and Results.* Vancouver, BC; University of British Columbia. 2009. Report.

Barton, David, et al. *Literacy Lives and Learning.* London: Routledge, 2007. Print.

Belzer, Alisa. "What Are They Doing in There? Case Studies of Volunteer Tutors and Adult Literacy Learners." *Journal of Adolescent and Adult Literacy*, 49.7 (2006): 560-572. Print.

Belzer, Alisa. "Less May Be More: Rethinking Adult Literacy Volunteer Tutor Training." *Journal of Literacy Research* 38.2 (2006): 111-140. Print.

Bell, Sherry Mee, Mary Ziegler, and R. Steve McCallum. "What Adult Educators Know Compared with What They Say They Know about Providing Research-based Reading Instruction." *Journal of Adolescent and Adult Literacy* 47.7 (2004): 542-563. Print.

Berry, Barnett. "What It Means to Be a "Highly Qualified Teacher." 2003. Southeast Center for Teaching Quality. Web.

Brick, Kate et al. *Refugee Resettlement in the United States: An Examination of Challenges and Proposed Solutions.* 2010. New York: Columbia University School of International and Public Affairs. Report.

Ceprano, Maria A. "Strategies and Practices of Individuals Who Tutor Adult Illiterates Voluntarily." *Journal of Adolescent and Adult Literacy* 39.1 (1995): 56-64. Print.

Chisman, Forrest P. *Closing the Gap: The Challenge of Certification and Credentialing in Adult Education.* 2011. New York: Council for Advancement of Adult Literacy. Report.

Crandall, JoAnn. "Creating a Professional Workforce in Adult ESL Literacy." ERIC Digest. 1994. Web.

Kerwin, Donald M. *The Faltering U.S. Refugee Protection System: Legal and Policy Responses to Refugees, Asylum Seekers, and Others in Need of Protection.* 2011. New York: Migration Policy Institute. Web.

McKenna, Rosa, and Lynne Fitzpatrick. *Building Sustainable Adult Literacy Provision: A Review of International Trends in Adult Literacy Policy and Programs.* 2004. Australia: The National Centre for Vocational Education Research. Web.

Muth, William, and Kristen Perry. "Adult Literacy: An Inclusive Framework." *Handbook of Research on Teaching the English Language Arts, Third Edition*. Eds. Diane Lapp and Douglas Fisher. New York: Routledge, 2010. 76-82. Print.

Perry, Kristen. *Adult Literacy and ESL Provision in Lexington.* 2010. Lexington, KY: Collaborative Center on Literacy Development. Report.

Perry, Kristen, and Susan Hart. "'I'm Just Kind of Winging It': Preparing & Supporting Educators of Adult Refugee Learners." *Journal of Adolescent and Adult Literacy* (2012): 110-122. Print.

Perry, Kristen, and Christine Mallozzi. "'Are You ABLE...to Learn?': Power and Access to Higher Education for African Refugees in the U.S." *Power and Education* 3 (2011): 249-262. Print.

Shulman, Lee. "Those Who Understand: Knowledge Growth in Teaching." *Educational Researcher* 15.2 (1986): 4-14. Print.

Suda, Liz. *Discourses of Greyness and Diversity: Revisiting the ALBE and ESL interface.* 2002. Victoria, Australia: Adult Literacy and Numeracy Australian Research Consortium. Web.

USCRI. (2010). "Engaging Communities: Preferred Communities Program." *U.S. Committee for Refugees and Immigrants*. USCRI, 2010. Web. 27 July, 2010.

Ziegler, Mary, R. Steve McCallum and Sherry Mee Bell. "Volunteer Instructors in Adult Literacy: Who Are They and What Do They Know About Reading Instruction?" *Adult Basic Education and Literacy Journal* 3.3 (2009): 131-139.

Kristen H. Perry is an assistant professor of literacy education at the University of Kentucky. She has investigated literacy practices among Sudanese refugees and educational opportunities for adult refugees. She co-directs the Cultural Practices of Literacy Study.

Literacy as an Act of Creative Resistance: Joining the Work of Incarcerated Teaching Artists at a Maximum-Security Prison

Anna Plemons

Considering the situated complexities and competing interest of exploitation and hope inherent in community literacy work, this article examines the ways that the Community Arts Program (CAP) at California State Prison-Sacramento complicates and also reifies archetypal grand literacy narratives and considers the place of such narratives within a broader argument for *literacy as acts of creative resistance* scaffolded by small, organic, tactical moves.

> *Literacy is valuable—and volatile—property ... a grounds for potential exploitation, injustice, and struggle as well as potential hope, satisfactions and reward. Wherever literacy is learned and practiced, these competing interests will always be present.*
>
> —Deborah Brant, Literacy in American Lives

Spoon Jackson played Pozzo in the 1987 San Quentin production of *Waiting for Godot*. Jackson's performance in *Godot* was preceded by his enrollment, in 1985, in a non-credit bearing poetry course taught by Judith Tannenbaum. Twenty-seven years later he teaches poetry at California State Prison-Sacramento (CSP-Sac) where he is serving a life-without-parole sentence. Last summer, when I was a guest teacher in his classroom, I asked him to sign a copy of *By Heart*, the book he co-authored with Tannenbaum.

Jackson's literacy narrative seems to reify the well-worn literacy myth of "have-nots" aligning themselves with academic sponsors to move from powerlessness to a place of economic viability and autonomy. A close look at the space in which Jackson finds himself as a writer and teacher is an appropriate starting point for building an argument that takes into consideration the situated complexities and "competing interest" of exploitation and hope that Deborah Brant notes are always present where literacy is "learned and practiced." Drawing on the work of Brant, as well as Kirk Branch, and Jeffrey Grabill, I will look closely at the ways that the Community Arts Program (CAP) at CSP-Sac – where Jackson teaches –complicates and also reifies archetypal grand literacy narratives. Furthermore, I will use the specific example of CAP to build a larger argument about community literacy sites – one that aims for *literacy as acts of creative resistance* scaffolded by small, organic, tactical moves. Thinking about literacy sites as organic, tactical spaces *without* an eye toward the strategic is important for a few key reasons.

Tactical moves are made by those without power (de Certeau). When programs move towards institutionalization (and strategic power) they inevitably move away from the margins, and the voices of those without power are subsumed. Thinking about literacy as an act of creative resistance fundamentally requires that the resistor retain ownership of – or agency over – the program. Secondly, the institutionalization of literacy programs sets them on a trajectory – establishes momentum – that almost always becomes self-serving. People are employed who then expect paychecks. Infrastructure grows. And infrastructure is always hungry for more infrastructure. The genuine support of creative, resistive literacy acts demands a type of space – a type of moment – that is not endangered by the births and deaths of the literacy acts themselves.

I want to focus on the literacy community but realize the impossibility of distancing myself from institutions in general, and (in this case) the totalizing institution of prison (Grabill 2). Making a case for organic, tactical moves inside (but at least in some ways distinct from) the institution is tightrope work. Grabill sees the need to view communities and institutions as mutually reinforcing, suggesting that if we do not see literacy as situated within these communities/institutions, we will be unable to spot the ways that local people and places construct alternative literacies (117).

That being said, recognizing the situated nature of local literacy practices is not the same as conceding all agency to the institution or supporting the creeping institutionalization of organic, tactical literacy practices and communities where they spring up. Essential to Grabill's argument is the clear articulation of ethics for any sponsor of literacy. Anyone who endeavors to commit themselves to such an effort must be clear on the "how," "why," and "with whom" of their commitment (53). Lorie Goodman reiterates: "Our grounds for action must remain under revision. We can never suppose that we are 'just' serving; we must always ask, 'In the service of what and whom?'" (Mathieu 93). This clarity, of course, leads back to a clear-eyed view of the institution in which the literacy practice or community is being established.

The connection between institution and community that Grabill suggests functions primarily by way of literacy sponsors, defined by Brant as "agents, local or distant, concrete or abstract, who enable, support, teach, and model, as well as recruit, regulate, suppress, or withhold, literacy – and gain advantage by it in some way" (19). In this study, CAP is the direct literacy sponsor, but Brant's notion of a sponsor is complicated by the context in which CAP operates. At present, CAP facilitates non-credit bearing creative writing and poetry classes in addition to a wider set of courses in visual arts, music theory, and performance. The most recent version of CAP sponsorship is difficult to situate bureaucratically – it is currently staffed under the umbrella of mental health with additional program materials coming from the Inmate Welfare Fund which supports inmate self-help programing (such as AA, NA, Toastmasters, etc.). CAP employs four inmate clerks who teach and organize the class offerings. Furthermore, in any given year, dozens of volunteer artists from outside the institution come in as guest teachers and performers, working with the incarcerated teachers who teach the bulk of the classes. Thus the sponsorship for the program is, in some ways, loose and difficult to define.

Because CAP facilitates relationships across race, class, and gender and makes attempts to mediate the clearly unequal relationships of power between members of the community, the work of Brant, Branch, and Grabill offer important theoretical framing for the study. However, because the Community Arts Program exists inside a maximum-security prison it requires an additional lens that takes into account the specific histories, limits and implications of working inside. To that end, I will look to Alexander, Cleveland, Cummins, Davis, Gilmore, Hartnett, Jackson, Lawston and Lucas, Meiners, Rusche and Kirchheimer, and Tannenbaum to articulate the constraints and possibilities of literacy work inside.

Moral Ambiguity, Trickster, and Prison Myth

It would be ill-conceived to begin talking about CAP as a site of creative, resistive literacy without recognizing that the literacy sponsorship for the program is bound up in the specific context of a particular maximum-security prison, inside the wider prison-industrial complex, inside the political economy that allows and encourages its growth. We can read about prison, and work to understand the systemic operations that explain how prison came to be, why is it growing like crazy, and who stands to benefit; but bringing the systemic critique to ground level often obscures a real, representative description of prison work.

Branch, who has taught inside, understands the obscured and situated nature of the prison classroom (10). He nonetheless makes a case for "carving out space to act," even within the systems that "appear so restrictive as to almost determine action" (12). He suggests that rather than "claiming to work for ends separate from the institutions we teach in (an impossible ideal), we need theories of pedagogy that allow for moral action in morally ambiguous contexts," suggesting a resistive agency that shapes even as it is itself shaped (11). Branch: "A teacher in a prison is never apart from that prison, and never apart from the penal system and the criminal justice system either" (93). In that sobering context, Branch creates some wiggle-room for individual agency by evoking the trickster figure who, by definition, functions in places of moral ambiguity (189). The trickster, in the case of the prison classroom, is drawn by Miles Horton's "magnetic pull of the *ought to be*" (Branch 18).

In *Trickster Makes This World: Mischief, Myth and Art*, Lewis Hyde describes the boundary-crossing trickster who acts without the paralysis of a totalizing moral judgment over the sacred work at hand. Trickster tales describe the double movement of hegemony – maintaining boundaries and simultaneously allowing ruptures (13). Trickster as agent is the "character in myth who threatens to take the myth apart" (14). About the goings on of prison there is much myth, myth that supports the status quo and myths created in opposition to it. Myths about prison fills the cavernous spaces where words would go if we knew how to talk about the complications and contradictions of the place; it seems impossible, or at least daunting to go looking for the words that substantively communicate what CSP-Sac is really like, or explain why I would choose to do work there that is in perpetual danger of supporting a profoundly oppressive system.

So, since I cannot claim the role of sage or all-seeing eye, in this essay I claim the role of witness. I am not the trickster who creates agency and bends the rules behind bars; the trickster teachers and tactically savvy administrators who make CAP work will be introduced later. I start my work as witness the only way I know how – with a memory.

Witness Work: Making a Case for Work Inside the Prison-Industrial Complex

My first experience on the yard at CSP-Sac was as a guest, invited to a concert made up of inmate Jazz bands, each with a coach from the outside. I tried to hold as still as possible, only moving my eyes to survey the bizarre scene – concrete everywhere, brittle grass, bent backs in oversized prison denim with bold block letters, army green officers with black sunglasses, and signs that said "NO WARNING SHOTS WILL BE FIRED." – I was ten miles from home on another planet. My escort leaned over and began overlaying the scene with important details. "See that guy at the mic – he is the number two Kumi on this yard. Kumi, the Swahili word for "ten" is the sum of four plus one plus five – and the name for a powerful prison-instigated Bay Area gang. And see the guy next to him, he's a Southern." Historically, C-Facility had been a site of violence between Black and Southern Mexican gang members. Entire cellblocks had been locked down for yearlong stretches. And recently, a guard had been stabbed.

The more I listened the more I understood that prison, already obscured from the public eye and all but severed from public memory, is complicated in ways that I, an observer, would never come to understand. It is full of violence and some "seriously sick shit," as one inmate recently told me. But, as evidenced by the concert I was attending, it could also be a site of creative resistance. At one point, I sat down within conversational range of two inmates. We talked about the upcoming parole of one man who had been inside since the year I was born. He explained to me that "two hundred bucks and a bus ticket" was going to be a rough transition.

The bus ticket story fits easily into a narrative web of scholars and practitioners like Angela Davis, Ruth Wilson Gilmore, Eric Cummins, Stephen Hartnett, Erica Meiners, Howard Winant, Victor Villanueva, Charles Mills, Marc Mauer, Georg Rusche, Otto Kirchheimer, and Buzz Alexander. Some speak directly to the political economy which is feeding the insatiable prison system on a steady diet of U. S. citizens. Others describe the landscape in less overtly materialist terms, but cannot seem to altogether escape noticing the heavy clouds that rain acid "justice" disproportionately on poor urban neighborhoods.

Ruth Wilson Gilmore points out that 60 percent of California's prisoners come from a five-county region in and around greater Los Angeles. This means that the State of California has committed to spending 60 percent of its billions of correctional dollars every year on selected men and women from a relatively small geographic area. Those dollars, however, are attached to the bodies of these people, which mean they are spent all along the I-5 corridor in converted farmland, not in the urban neighborhoods that so clearly need support.

The insane lack of human logic that surrounds the prison-industrial complex (PIC) turns my stomach. It has also brought scholars and activists from a variety of disciplines to the Prison Abolition Movement, loosely defined here as a set of strategies and positions focused on loosening the corporate clutch of capitalism on U.S.

systems of punishment, in large part by stemming the tide of people being sucked into the system. Thinking again about Los Angeles and all that is lost when generations are chained, bused, and scattered across the central valley is motivation enough to join the cause. Communities are hemorrhaging. And the blood that is lost shows up on the evening news as a conformation of pervasive "tough on crime" anti-logic.

There is ample evidence that "tough on crime" really means surveillance and punishment of the poor. Christian Parenti uses examples from New Jersey and Massachusetts to point out that those in the drug trade who can afford to, pay their way out of the system with their illegal profits, thus avoiding mandatory sentencing and the spectacle of the courtroom. The discrepancies between sentencing for powder and crack cocaine are well known. And then there are the stories like Enron. Punishment does not linearly follow crime.

For that reason, the stories and numbers offered by scholars like Gilmore and Parenti need to find a place in the conversation. Almost nobody I know in prison thinks that prisons should go away. There are people whose violent and/or deviant acts violate the social contract in ways that justify imprisonment. But that reality does not account for the exponential increase in the use of incarceration in the United States, or the ways that class and race based policing and judicial practices disproportionately target poor, urban neighborhoods.

Considering the momentum with which the PIC grows and the scope of its effect on the poor, a radical prison abolitionist position argues against opportunities for inmates, assuming that such opportunities serve the system, or to state it in more vulgar terms, placate the slaves on America's new plantation. At the same time, I argue that scholars, activists, and particularly teachers can (and must) work from inside and outside the PIC in tactical, organic, critically resistive ways despite the moral ambiguity that surrounds the work.

So what can tactical, organic, critically resistive literacy look like? As Stephen Hartnett articulates, a critical resistance that aims at empowerment, community building and social change, can – no *must* – incorporate the aesthetic and the pedagogical alongside the political. It is not enough to take an ideological political position. Likewise, teaching in the prison or encouraging creative endeavors without an eye towards critical resistance (both of dehumanizing systems and personal processes) is in danger of continuing a long history of control and manipulation under the guise of "rehabilitation."

I suggest that prison classrooms (where inmate teachers, for example, facilitate literacy alongside a wider offering of the arts) are sites with real tactical purpose and import. If the people inside stop participating in organically constructed ways of their own choosing, the broader conversation about what do to with incarcerated people becomes abstracted in ways that are ultimately unhelpful and end up (re)commodifying incarcerated bodies as Eric Cummins (1994) points out is his treatise of the radical prison movement in California (discussed later).

There are myriad charts and graphs that explain the "what" of the PIC. There are even charts and graphs that deal with the "why" – threading its development to capitalistic agendas delivered through political mouthpieces and the evening news. But amid the charts and graphs there needs to be space for unlikely organic things to happen and space for prisoners (who choose) to reimagine themselves outside of their crime, even if that (re)imagining does not seem to change their material situation, at least not in ways that feel palatable to scholars looking in from the outside.

Beginning to (Re)Imagine: Big and Little Literacy Narratives in the CAP Program

When I teach at CSP-Sac, I am a guest in a few different writing classes and one intensive journaling group. I work with classes on both a mainline yard and in the mental health unit. Ducats, the roll call sheets that authorize inmates to attend, can have up to 20 people on them. But by the time the last writers trickle in, attendance is usually in the teens. Guards are not always eager to call inmates out of their "houses." Depending on the day of the week, some writers don't get called at all, since the gang violence between Northerns and Southerns precludes their use of the yard on the same days.

Incarcerated writers have described the CAP room, where classes meet, as safe and sacred space. They talk of taking off their armor when they enter, and speak of the even more arduous process of putting it back on when they leave. They describe the portal as a time-space continuum of sorts and sometimes talk about how the jarring of coming and going can be too much; sometimes writers choose not to come, any gains weighed against the pain of leaving.

In the room, I am learning, there is code of safety that makes space for each writer's work, even when it reifies the dominant narrative. We offer comment and critique for each other, but we also allow writers to write from the place where they stand. Grabill says it this way: "Programs and teachers cannot force critical consciousness after all, nor can they minimize personal and/or functional needs" (113). Barging in with a narrowly defined agenda is both unproductive and profoundly disrespectful.

Sometimes writers draw from a place of thinly veiled fiction. Often, especially when writers are new to the class, the writing fits neatly into clichéd prison genres – memoirs from the street or poems about the steamy lady who is waiting back home. Sometimes the writing is real, raw, and thoughtful. Sometimes it is combative – explosions orchestrated by razor sharp intellect. I take my cues from the group whose default posture is a *patient knowing* based on years of watching new writers inevitably feel the need to say some of the same old things on their way to saying something new. Writers offer each other suggestions and challenges that sometimes start heated conversations that zig and zag through race, class, gender, and politics. The exchanges that are made are made with the coin of the realm – scraps of public writing. Everyone who comes, writes. Most who come, read aloud. And each public offering is wrapped in a *patient knowing* that each man has to wait for his own word.

This *patient knowing* somewhat overlaps with Paul Loeb's "radical patience" described by Paula Mathieu in *Tactics of Hope: The Public Turn in Composition*. Mathieu summarized Loeb's idea as the "ability to remain engaged in the messy, unpredictable process of public participation without burning out or becoming cynical" (47). I have watched incarcerated writers responding to each other with this long-term vision and have tried to likewise adopt the posture. The violence and control of a maximum-security prison make it predictably unpredictable. The moral ethic of Grabill requires that teachers in this space be ever sure of their intentions, and careful with the power they wield. This added to Branch's realistic articulation regarding the moral ambiguity essential to prison makes for a volatile cocktail. A respect for the work of CAP requires that teaching guests adopt the local turn towards radical patience – both with the other writers in the circle and with all (read *nearly everything*) that is out of the control of those who make the program work. Bringing impatience to this place threatens its very existence.

As a guest (and even as a sponsor) of this local literacy community, I forfeit the "right" to unreflectively speak my mind to the guards who are also caught up in this maddening ecosystem. Appreciating the delicate, tactical nature of what CAP is attempting to do requires a patience that often chooses small actions instead of big ones, or sometimes (what appears to be) no action at all. The politics of the prison ecosystem seems absurd at best and cruel and arbitrary at worst. I have seen volunteers come into the institution and immediately adopt a "change agent" posture that seems focused on the material conditions of inmates, but, I would argue is often times, at bottom, an unreflective coping strategy for processing their PIC experience. Unreflective action on the part of volunteers can dangerously subsume the articulated desires of inmates, ending with volunteers making decisions for which inmates are ultimately disciplined (Cummins). The rules of the PIC may, over time, be negotiated, but they cannot be ignored, because when they are, the punishment comes back – every time – on the incarcerated men and women who choose to risk community partnership.

When I teach I am a guest in classes usually taught by Spoon Jackson and Marty Williams, both of whom are inmate teaching-artists and long-term CAP clerks (the title of clerk allows inmate teaching-artists to make prison wages while teaching and handling the administrative duties, like making ducats, that keep the program going). Spoon Jackson has been a teaching-artist at CSP-Sac for over eight years. He is currently in this thirty-fourth year of a life-without parole sentence. His first contact with CAP (then Arts in Corrections) was a poetry class taught by Judith Tannenbaum at San Quentin, an experience he writes about in *By Heart: Poetry, Prison and Two Lives*, the memoir he co-authored with Tannenbaum.

Jackson writes about how he showed up for Tannenbaum's poetry class and sat in silence, with his back to the wall in a ring of chairs he set up as a perimeter of defense. Then, after a year, he brought a stack of poems. And played Pozzo in "Waiting for Godot" at San Quentin in 1987. Then authored a book. And continues to write peer-reviewed articles that I can find at the campus library.

This bulleted list of Spoon's endeavors reads like the reifying salvation narrative so readily accessible, even in scholarly discourse. In *Right to Be Hostile*, Erica Mieners offers a poignant example from the genre: "I was born; I had problems; I made the wrong choices; I was apprehended by the police; I was incarcerated; I found God and He helped me. And…my life is now on a better track" (139). Eve Ensler's 2003 documentary, "What I Want My Words To Do To You: Voices from a Maximum-Security Women's Prison" unwittingly offers a glaringly flat-footed window into the composing of salvation narratives. Ensler designs writing prompts that continually situation writers inside their crime, encouraging remorse and individual responsibility. At multiple points she talks over writers as they are explaining or reading their work, making suggestions about their feelings and their experiences with their families. Even when writers push back or dismiss her inappropriate over-stepping, she does not change directions. Ensler's PBS documentary is representative of the genre that Meiners and others have openly critiqued. Critics of the salvation narrative script rightly find that it is wholly inappropriate for literacy sponsorship to delineate the socio-emotional boundaries of the writer.

For me, however, narratives like that of Jackson significantly complicate the genre, calling for a "both/and" space where incarcerated writers have the freedom to tell their stories as they see it, even when those tellings seem to come back around to worn out myths. In *By Heart* Jackson describes the scenes (prison library, prison classroom, and prison theatre production) where he "finds his voice" and credits reading and writing with bringing a sense of purpose and creative outlet that helps him reimagine himself (or at least get back to what was lost early in his public schooling). He writes: "I learned a few new words each day and each one brought a geyser erupting inside my mind and soul. The more I read and studied, the clearer life became. I became richer and deeper inside . . . I had to till the endless gardens in my mind, heart, and soul" (2). Of the library years before he began attending poetry class he writes: "For eight years I had stayed to myself at San Quentin, learning who I was and what I was about. I avoided crowds. Although my heart, mind and soul burned with thoughts, vibes, and feelings, I let none surface and stepped over wounded, dying, or dead bodies as everyone else did" (2). Jackson writes of his expectations about the poetry course: he was sure he would not like it, considering poetry to be the realm of "women, squares, nerds, weirdoes, professors, and highbrows, people caught up in some unreal academic world" (2).

But he *does* begin to write. And writing does change – in small, organic, tactical ways – his material situation. He becomes a published writer and teacher. And more recently, when offered the opportunity to move to a different institution where he could more closely align himself with a university, he chose to stay at CSP-Sac, calling the program he has helped build "a mecca for the arts." Jackson navigates impossibly narrow constraints without strategic control over some of his most basic needs. And yet he gets to decide (for the moment) whether or not to move from one institution to another, weighing his opportunities as a teaching artist in each place. With Jackson in mind, I find support for the articulation that writing and teaching bring some small agency and serve to alleviate (to some extent) the oppressiveness of doing "life without."

Thinking about the way that Jackson moves inside the prison, creating spaces and moments that transcend incarceration, calls up the image of the trickster with parallels between Jackson's literacy narrative and Hyde's analysis of the literacy narrative of Frederick Douglass. In *Trickster* Hyde uses the trickster myth to situate the life of Frederick Douglass. Hyde concedes that "a person as serious and moralizing as Frederick Douglass" does not seem to embody the trickster myth, but takes up some trickster qualities because he is so clearly situated on the margins (226). Douglass was born into a deeply conflicted moral system, a system in which he adopts the Hermetic position of theft. He "steals" literacy from his father who is unwilling to give it, and that stealing of literacy leads Douglass to see, in his own words, a "pathway from slavery to freedom" (228). Hyde suggests that the acts of reading and writing, when performed by Douglass, are acts that "undercut plantation culture" (229). Hyde continues: "If Douglass hopes to be the active disenchanter of his master's world, he must speak and write" not just to any public, but specifically to a white public – the public of his oppressor (229). This speaking across the color line, this breaking of the rules of silence, this contestation of the "white world's fictions about slavery" leads Douglass to articulate a sense of freedom. The quality of the silence that Douglass must break runs parallel through Jackson's narrative. Choosing to write, for both men, is a choice against silence and a move towards public engagement with the oppressor (and/or his proxy). And in both instances breaking silence through literacy fundamentally disrupts (or at least disorients) the well-tended hegemonic fiction.

Hyde's analysis of Douglass also exposes complications to the Frederick Douglass literacy myth where all ends well for those who learn to read and write. Douglass *does* gain some tactical (and maybe even strategic) power in his lifetime. But, as Hyde points out, despite the fact that Douglass lives to see much of plantation culture collapse, no utopic phoenix rises from its ashes: "Yankee culture [has] its own organizing divisions, some of them odious and remarkably indelible" (237). Looking back on his own life, Douglass writes in his 1855 autobiography about his youthful enthusiasm in adopting a good cause with good people; with the encouragement of his white supporters, Douglass speaks and writes to and for an audience and is "made to forget that my skin was dark and my hair crisped" (quoted in Hyde 243). This close circle of white supporters "prompted, sanctioned, introduced and authorized Douglass's voice; they were also his sympathetic listeners" (245).

Hyde describes him as a man "moving from speechlessness into speech as he enters what he thought was a world organized to include him" (246). But time proved otherwise and in the eventual writings of the *Frederick Douglass' Paper*, he is described by African American readers as finally developing a "colored" voice: "I have read his paper very carefully and find phrase after phrase develop itself as in one newly born among us" (247). Douglass's literacy moves from aligning with his early literacy sponsors to choosing to pursue what Hyde calls an "essential self" in the voice of the *Frederick Douglass' Paper*. This movement charts a course through a profound disillusionment with his lack of true membership in the white circle of his literacy sponsors.

Douglass as Trickster: Literacy Sponsorship and Tactical Moves

I want to make the case that Douglass uses literacy in tactical, organic and nuanced ways that resonate both with Jackson's story and the underlying principles of the CAP program. Douglass starts with a salvation narrative of sorts which catches the imagination of his literacy sponsors, who (intentionally or not) co-opt and attempt to censor his story as well as directly manage its telling. Douglass: "It was impossible for me to repeat the same old story, month after month, and to keep up my interest . . . 'Tell your story, Frederick,' would whisper my revered friend, Mr. Garrison, as I stepped upon the platform. I could not always follow the injunction, for I was now reading and thinking" (243).

So Douglass – Hyde's trickster at the threshold of possibility – leans hard against the edges of hegemony. This is the same dangerous ground where incarcerated writers like Jackson and his students find themselves. They are sponsored to a point, and that point – that edge – is the focus of much of the extreme prison abolitionist debate. What is the real use of tactical power? Can literacy programs inside maximum-security prisons be anything other that a grand and cruel placation of America's new slaves? What is really to be gained by incarcerated men and women who choose to read and bravely write their own story?

Proponents of programs like CAP talk about (re)discovering humanity. Opponents of such programs argue that a discovery of humanity without the material gain of physical freedom is at best a sham and at worst a deep violence. But, when the organic, tactical opportunity for discovery exists within a person, there is also violence in working against such men and women, working as they are to rupture the big and small lies they carry and bring a bit of a silenced soul to the surface. Douglass's story does not really begin with a salvation narrative; it begins with his pursuit of something that was being strategically withheld from him. So he pursues literacy, finds sponsors, writes a salvation narrative, outgrows the space that once felt free and moves for the first time into a voice that is his own.

Hyde writes that after 1847 Douglass no longer "forgets" his dark skin and crisped hair. "He becomes black, reimaging his family history and redirecting his voice to a more receptive audience" (247). Hyde suggests that this is a reluctant rebirth brought on by Douglass's profound tiring of the trope of the self-education savage. The liminal space between man and his trope suffocates, "but what were his choices? If there is no way to stay poised on the edge, which is the better fate, cannibalism or anthropemy, to be eaten by ideology or vomited into exile? Unless he wanted to leave the country, he would have to work with the hand that history had dealt" (248).

Therein lies the fundamental seat of contradiction for literacy sponsorship in places likes a maximum-security prison where the literacy myth of economic gain does not hold. The teachers I know at CSP-Sac are serving life-without-parole sentences. Barring some cataclysmic event they will leave prison in body bags – either by violence or old age. They can choose organic, tactical moves inside the belly of the beast but their choices will not lead to physical freedom. Their choices can, and often do, offer a measure of agency in a near-totalizing institution. And such agency has real value, even if it is tactical and contingent.

Agency and Sponsorship: Getting to the Specific Context of CAP

Fundamental to an organic, tactical position is the understanding that the people inside can (and must) participate in organically constructed ways of their own choosing. Broadly, if teachers like Jackson and Williams stop teaching, and the writers they are working with stop writing and speaking in public and semi-public spaces, the outside conversation about what do to with incarcerated people becomes abstracted in ways that are ultimately unhelpful and end up (re)commodifying incarcerated bodies. In his book, *The Rise and Fall of California's Radical Prison Movement*, Cummins goes into great detail about how the Bay Area Left's co-option of the *hyper-sexualized inmate outlaw* ended up disrupting community support for inmate-initiated reform at San Quentin. The situation Cummins describes is highly complicated with lots of moving parts, but what is clear, even at a surface level, is that incarcerated writers fostered connections with the Bay Area Left based on the promise (or at least the imagining) of a strategic alliance. The incarcerated writers at San Quentin mistook the Left's interest for real, material opportunity. By the bloody end, the community writ large had withdrawn its support for inmates, yet probably never really understood what it was that they were asking for. The drama calls back the details of Frederick Douglass's experience with white sponsorship of his abolitionist agenda.

Understanding the messy and impossibly contradictory nature of prison politics, CAP works to circumvent a strategic political agenda. It also rejects outright the notion of rehabilitation (the "R" word) with its terrifying history of abuse. Without a political or rehabilitative agenda, CAP chooses to narrow its own articulation of itself to this: basic opportunities to do creative work in community. This seemingly small agenda inside the massive machine of the PIC seems almost laughably foolish. But the lack of hubris is quite possibly the very thing that has allowed the program to exist amid the twin extremes of violence and control that define prison.

As tactical and organic as it may be, CAP does require sponsorship. As Grabill understands, a program like CAP must have "an insider," an agent with considerable institutional power (141). At one point, what is now CAP was called Arts in Corrections, a statewide program with a state employee at each institution serving in the dual role of teaching-artists and bureaucratic insider. CAP has retained, for the moment, a version of that position. And the person who holds it understands that what CAP fundamentally requires is a rupturing of sorts in the dominating, oppressive social relations that are standard in prison. Mathieu moves towards recognizing the well-timed dance of the bureaucratic insider when she takes up the work of Iris Marion Young (1990) and William M. Sullivan (1995). Young reframes rights more as *doing* than as *having*, a position in keeping with de Certeau's original statements about tactics belonging to those without "real" material power. Sullivan makes a bit more room for the agency of the insider, suggesting that although "institutions make certain practices possible and others impossible . . . individuals can also change institutional orders" (122).

Mathieu continues to speak to CAP's seemingly small, tactical agenda – offering basic opportunities to do creative work in community – in her framing of tactical work as grounded in a hope characterized by a "critical, active, dialectical engagement between the insufficient present and possible, alternative futures" (xv). Her claims about what tactical work should look like and what it should be aiming for call back to Miles Horton's "eye on the ought to be." She suggests that tactical projects "accomplish only themselves" (xix). Mathieu:

> One works for and hopes for change in the powerful systems that script our society, but one does not look to transactional rewards as a needed extrinsic exchange for the act of writing. The doing of the thing itself has to be enough pleasure or reward, because being heard in a fractured pub-

lic and making change in the world is a slow and unpredictable process. (47)

Mathieu understands that organic, tactical work seems to aim low, and even when its sail *does* catch a breeze and fly, it does not expect that it has become a bird.

I attended a debriefing meeting in November where Williams and a few other teaching-artists met with a band of visiting musicians who had spent six days inside. This was the seventh year that they had made the trip from Alaska to California. Those particular musicians bring an energy to the CAP program that opens up spaces that close again when they leave. Williams thanked the artists for coming and described his personal process for dealing with the coming and going of volunteers. And I, as witness, heard again the same thing Williams has been telling me for years – that a tactical orientation allows him and the other teaching-artists agency in an otherwise totalizing place.

I end this witness back where I began, with three scholars who speak directly to the dangers, contradictions and ambiguities of literacy acts, literacy communities, and literacy teaching in a maximum-security prison. Brant calls for a framing of literacy that understands that it is always situated. Branch calls on Horton as he makes the case that "to work towards something that seems impossible to realize is not the mark of a futile activity" (11). Literacy sponsorship that operates primarily through tactical and organic means in the morally ambiguous context of a maximum-security prison does (and should) give us pause. But a clear-headed and well-informed look at the institution of prison does not need to preclude tactical work from inside the system.

Teachers, in any institution, who continue to show up day after day cannot escape some belief in individual agency. Branch claims, and I agree, that all classrooms where literacy practices are taught (or supported) ascribe some agency to those literacy practices. "Educational literacy practices are supposed to take students beyond the literacy practices already familiar to them when they enter the classroom. Why else would we presume to teach? (214). We do teach. And for most of us, an unresolvable moral ambiguity will always accompany the work (216).

Williams says that before there was CAP he was playing his guitar against the wall on the yard. What Williams and other incarcerated teaching-artists I know will say is that literacy, defined here as acts of creative resistance, will be part of the prison fabric, whether or not it is scaffolded by the organic, tactical support of bureaucratic insiders and volunteer teachers. The question is not whether or not these literacy communities make sense to outsiders, but whether or not they find support to function in the ways of their choosing.

Works Cited

Alexander, Michelle. *The New Jim Crow: Mass Incarceration in the Age of Colorblindness*. 1st ed. The New Press, 2010. Print.

Alexander, William. *Is William Martinez Not Our Brother?: Twenty Years of the Prison Creative Arts Project*. University of Michigan Press, 2010. Print.

Branch, Kirk. *"Eyes on the Ought to Be": What We Teach About When We Teach About Literacy*. Hampton Press, 2007. Print.
Brandt, Deborah. *Literacy as Involvement: The Acts of Writers, Readers, and Texts*. 1st ed. Southern Illinois University Press, 1990. Print.
_____. *Literacy in American Lives*. 1st ed. Cambridge University Press, 2001. Print.
Certeau, Michel de. *The Practice of Everyday Life*. 2nd ed. University of California Press, 2002. Print.
Cleveland, William, and Patricia Allen Shifferd. *Between Grace and Fear: The Role of the Arts in a Time of Change*. Common Ground Publishing, 2010. Print.
Cole, Daniel. "Writing removal and resistance: Native American rhetoric in the composition classroom." *College Composition and Communication* 63.1 (2011): 122-144. Print.
Cummins, Eric. *The Rise and Fall of California's Radical Prison Movement*. 1st ed. Stanford University Press, 1994. Print.
Davis, Angela Y. *Abolition Democracy: Beyond Empire, Prisons, and Torture*. Seven Stories Press, 2005. Print.
_____. *Are Prisons Obsolete?* Seven Stories Press, 2003. Print.
Flower, Linda. *Community Literacy and the Rhetoric of Public Engagement*. 1st ed. Southern Illinois University Press, 2008. Print.
Freire, Paulo. *Pedagogy of the Oppressed*. 30th ed. Continuum, 2000. Print.
Frost, Alanna. "Literacy stewardship: Dakelh women composing culture." *College Composition and Communication* 63.1 (2011): 54-74. Print.
Gaucher, Robert. *Writing as Resistance: The Journal of Prisoners on Prisons Anthology (1988-2002)*. Toronto, Ont. : Canadian Scholars' Press, 2002. Print.
Gilmore, Ruth Wilson. *Golden Gulag: Prisons, Surplus, Crisis, and Opposition in Globalizing California*. 1st ed. University of California Press, 2007. Print.
Grabill, Jeffrey T. *Community Literacy Programs and the Politics of Change*. State Univ of New York Pr, 2001. Print.
Hartnett, Stephen John. *Challenging the Prison-Industrial Complex: Activism, Arts, and Educational Alternatives*. 1st ed. University of Illinois Press, 2010. Print.
Horton, Myles, and Paulo Freire. *We Make The Road by Walking: Conversations on Education and Social Change*. Temple University Press, 1990. Print.
Hyde, Lewis. *Trickster Makes This World: Mischief, Myth, and Art*. Farrar, Straus and Giroux, 2010. Print.
Jackson, Spoon. "Speaking in Poems." *Teaching Artist Journal* 5.1 (2007): 22. Print.
Lawston, Jodie Michelle, and Ashley E. Lucas. *Razor Wire Women: Prisoners, Activists, Scholars, and Artists*. State Univ of New York Pr, 2011. Print.
Masters, Jarvis Jay. *That Bird Has My Wings: The Autobiography of an Innocent Man on Death Row*. Reprint. Harper One, 2010. Print.
Mathieu, Paula. *Tactics of Hope: The Public Turn in English Composition*. Boynton/Cook, 2005. Print.
Meiners, Erica R. *Right to Be Hostile: Schools, Prisons, and the Making of Public Enemies*. Routledge, 2007. Print.
Polanyi, Karl. *The Great Transformation: The Political and Economic Origins of Our Time*. 2nd ed. Beacon Press, 2001. Print.

Pompa, Lori. "Service-Learning as Crucible: Reflections on Immersion, Context, Power, and Transformation." *Michigan Journal of Community Service Learning* 9.1 (2002): 67-76. Print.

Powell, Malea. "Rhetorics of Survivance: How American Indians Use Writing." *College Composition and Communication* 53.3 (2002): 396. Print.

Rusche, Georg, and Otto Kirchheimer. *Punishment and Social Structure*. Revised. Transaction Publishers, 2003. Print.

Tannenbaum, Judith. *Disguised As A Poem: My Years Teaching at San Quentin*. First Printing. Northeastern, 2000. Print.

Villanueva, Victor. *Bootstraps: From an American Academic of Color*. Natl Council of Teachers, 1993. Print.

Anna Plemons is a guest teaching-artist at California State Prison-Sacramento. She is also a PhD candidate in Rhetoric and Composition at Washington State University where her primary research interests revolve around teaching and writing in prison, and the complications and implications of such work.

Constructing Adult Literacies at a Local Literacy Tutor-Training Program

Ryan Roderick

This study investigates how literacy was constructed at an adult literacy organization's volunteer tutor-training program. By drawing on qualitative analysis of training texts used during training, such as training evaluations, and data gathered from interviews with experienced tutors, it is possible to identify the assumptions about literacy constructed by the training program and tutors' training practices. Tutors seemed to present mixed assumptions about literacy: students simultaneously were given authority over their own literacy practices and literacy goals, while a sentiment of universally valued reading and writing skills was also present in terms of achieving fluency.

By way of introducing my use of the term literacy in this study, I want to address what Thomas Smith notes as two varying understandings. In Smith's review of governmental policies' assumptions about literacy, he notes that current definitions of literacy and learning are being "pushed and pulled in competing directions" (35). Literacy is "pushed" in the sense that an increasingly diverse student population is prompting educators to recognize those students' diverse ways of knowing as kinds of literacies. In addition, literacy is "pulled" in the sense that reforms to education, such as No Child Left Behind, have seemingly narrowed definitions of literacy to a standard, universally applicable set of reading and writing skills. It is this pushing and pulling of literacy that I want to introduce, because I am curious about where community literacy organizations might fit within these two very different sets of assumptions about literacy.

Recent research into literacy practices of student writers shows reading and writing abilities as inseparable from social, cultural, and generic contexts (Gee; Prior & Shipka; Berkenkotter et al.). Such an understanding of literacies as multiple and varied relative to their socio-cultural context suggests that teachers recognize the growing diversity of their students' varying reading and writing abilities. Brian Street and others refer to the understanding that literacy is always connected to social and cultural contexts as *New Literacies*. The concept of New Literacies "represents a shift in perspective on the study and acquisition of literacy from the dominant cognitive model, with its emphasis on reading, to a broader understanding of literacy practices in their social and cultural contexts" (qtd. in Smith 41). While a New Literacies understanding of language acquisition may now be the paradigm in most first-year composition courses, little research has been done to examine what role, if any, a New Literacies paradigm takes in community literacy programs. In what ways might literacy, as it is constructed in composition studies, align or diverge from literacy as it is constructed in local community literacy programs, and what might this alignment or divergence mean for the work that community literacy tutors and students do? A 1998 survey of 271 literacy programs across forty-one states suggests that these programs largely understood being literate as ability with a fixed set of skills that, once learned, could then be applied regardless of the contexts in which they were used. According to the survey, 73% of adult literacy programs' instructional practices were somewhat to highly decontextualized and somewhat to highly teacher-directed (Purcell-Gates et al. 80-83).

However, adult literacy students are widely diverse in the purposes, skill sets, beliefs, and experiences they bring to their pursuit of literacy education (Greenberg). In light of Gee's and Russell's conclusions that reading and writing is always contextual, such a diverse population of adult literacy students suggests—as it did for Smith—that adult literacy tutors are working with a wide range of students and a variety of literacies rooted in an equally diverse range of social and cultural contexts. Such a climate of adult literacy education brings me back to my initial question: how are adult literacy programs constructing literacy given the complex climate created by emerging assumptions articulated as New Literacies and residual assumptions about literacy as a universally applicable set of skills?

A Review of Relevant Literature

Given the diversity of adult literacy students, and that many community literacy programs rely heavily on volunteers, student-centered pedagogies have been given some attention recently (Belzer; Godbee; Talarr). In addition, many community literacy programs train tutors to implement some version of a student-centered approach to tutoring. This approach has grown out of critical pedagogies, perhaps most notable of which is that developed by Freire. Student-centered approaches to tutoring structure learners' and tutors' roles/knowledges/abilities through an ongoing process of negotiation between two different sets of expertise, teacher and student. A student-centered approach means that tutors are expected to adapt their tutoring practices to further the goals and expertise of the particular learner they are working with (Talarr; Godbee). In addition, student-centered approaches to tutoring tend to work under the assumption that "literacy work [is] grounded in the life of the student," which is related to increased attendance rates and frequency or type of out-of-school literacy practices among students (Purcell-Gates et al. 74).

The move to student-centered tutoring has, however, posed some difficulty. Talarr noted that despite some attempts to train tutors in student-centered approaches, tutors tended to revert back to the teacher-directed strategies they themselves had been taught with as students (384). Similarly, when studying the assumptions about literacy constructed by one-on-one tutor and student pairs, Pomerance found that "despite the presentation of alternatives in the training, [volunteer tutors] tend to teach in conventional ways" (Abstract). In addition, Ceprano also noted that volunteer tutors, despite good intentions, tended to utilize instructional strategies that reflected their past experience as students, rather than the ones they encountered while being trained as a literacy tutor. Thus, Ceprano suggests volunteers find it difficult to develop productive tutoring strategies that overcome "feelings of frustration and defeat for their clients" (63). However, Talarr's experience using "active listening" as a training tool suggests that tutors may be prepared to reflect on and develop a productive student-centered approach (385).

As far as volunteer training goes, some researchers have advocated a "less is more" philosophy. In a study of one literacy program that focuses on children having difficulty reading, Baker et al. found "significant impact" on reading and writing skills of second graders despite receiving only one to two hours of training prior to being paired one-on-one with a student (510). Such little training was the result of a low-cost design, and it was believed that very little training would improve volunteer recruitment. However, since that study focuses on kindergarten through second grade students, it might be inaccurate to assume that such a training model could also be effective with volunteers tutoring adults. Belzer's findings suggest that tutor training might not always transfer to practice, which leads her to claim that less initial training and more ongoing training in order to help tutors develop skills to respond to the specific needs and strengths of students and tutors as they work together (133-134). In addition to these challenges of transfer, D'Amico and Schnee show that there are social and political barriers to using literacy skills, which tutors often perceive as separate from reading and writing skills (136). Given that social and cultural factors are also a part of using reading and writing in certain contexts to do certain things, their study suggests that volunteers also be trained to address such factors.

Research Questions

In this study, I take up Talarr's notion of training as a process that allows volunteers to move "beyond an ideology that focuses on learners' deficiencies to one that focuses on their strengths, in order to be able to help learners build on them" (384). That is, I look at tutor training and how it affects volunteers' disposition towards enacting a student-centered approach to tutoring. I ask the following research questions:
 1. What sets of assumptions about literacy and literacy tutoring are being put into action through adult literacy tutor-training programs?
 2. How does a student-centered approach to literacy tutoring affect the tutoring practices of volunteer literacy tutors who complete the training?

It is my hope that asking such questions will help uncover the ways literacy is being constructed at the local level. From there, I can speculate back on alignments with/divergences from New Literacies. The organization I studied trains tutors to work with both native and non-native English speakers. They offer two types of training, one of which they call "Basic Literacy" training, which prepares volunteers for work with native English speakers; and "English Language Learner" training, which prepares volunteers for work with non-native English speakers. In order to identify sets of assumptions about literacy being put into action through the organization, I draw on data from both programs.

Data Collection and Analysis

I looked at three sets of data from the volunteer tutor-training programs operating at a community literacy organization I am calling Eastern Adult Literacy[1] (EAL). EAL is a volunteer community literacy organization that serves a fifty-mile radius around a small city in the northeast U.S. They recruit and train volunteer literacy tutors to enact "learner-centered" tutoring. Following training, volunteers are paired one-on-one with adult learners. Meetings between tutors and learners typically occur once a week in pre-decided locations—e.g. libraries, cafés, etc.—and these meetings usually last about an hour. EAL runs two tutor-training programs: "Basic Literacy" and "English Language Learner" training. Basic Literacy training is meant to prepare volunteers to tutor adults whose primary language is English, while English Language Learner training, as its name suggests, is meant to prepare tutors to work with those for who English is a foreign language.

Drawing from Smith & Schryer's construct of "documentary society" (136), I mapped volunteers' experiences as they were structured by a series of documents that situated volunteers in a "local course of action" (145). That is, I attempted to capture the way certain institutional documents allowed volunteers to enter and move through EAL's tutor-training program (Appendix A). This construct allowed me to contextualize my data within an institutional role. The data I collected for this study included training evaluations from EAL's Basic Literacy and English Language Learner tutor-training programs; interviews I conducted with tutors who completed the training; and the training texts used in the Basic Literacy training course.

Training evaluations from training sessions—dating from 2009 to 2011—serve as records of volunteers' experience of the training as they were working through each of the five Basic Literacy training sessions. Each trainee completed an evaluation following each training session, thus it is likely that trainees' responses on evaluations in later sessions may have been affected in some way by their growing familiarity with the document. In addition, their use of the evaluation after each session may likely have influenced their experience of subsequent sessions. Since I received the results of these evaluations only after they had been compiled into spreadsheets, I was not able to account for these influences.

I used thirty-four English Language Learner (ELL) Tutor-Training Evaluations and twenty-seven Basic Literacy (BL) Tutor-Training Evaluations. Tutor-Training Evaluations prompt a numerical evaluation of tutor-training sessions as well as open-ended comments. Numerical evaluations ask trainees to rate aspects of the training, such as "objectives of workshop," "ideas and activities," and "overall content" on a scale of 1-5. Since these ratings tended not to ever fall below 4, I did not find the numerical ratings useful for this project. Instead, I focused specifically on the open-ended comments, since they referred to a variety of aspects of the training, and often provided critiques. Comments also showed a range of ways in which trainees were talking about literacy tutoring.

The open-ended comments on training evaluations documented a time when tutors were experiencing training, yet had not been paired with a learner. This allowed me to see ways in which the training was acting on trainees to construct an image of adult literacy tutoring. However, it did not allow me to see what image of adult literacy tutoring was taken up once tutors began tutoring. Knowing how adult literacy tutors were experiencing actual tutoring sessions would allow me to compare those experiences with those constructed by the training. In order to collect those experiences, I decided to conduct interviews with experienced literacy tutors.

I interviewed eight tutors who had each completed tutor training more than two years prior to the interview. I limited my selection to only those tutors who signed their name to the training evaluation. Such a selection was made because it could allow me to compare what tutors described in the interview with the kinds of comments they made on evaluations during training. Six out of eight tutors—75%— were female. Seven out of eight were over the age of 45—87%. All but one had prior teaching experience. My sample of informants, although smaller than I would have liked, is roughly representative of the general tutor population at EAL. In an unpublished report, EAL indicated that out the 279 volunteers, 222—80%—are female, and 205—73%—are ages forty-five and older. Although EAL does not track which tutors had prior teaching experience, my observation of the Basic Literacy training program conducted in February 2012 found that only two out of the fifteen trainees had prior teaching experience.

Interviews were conducted in person at a public location that the informant and I had decided upon prior to the interview. These interviews were recorded and transcribed for analysis. I followed a prepared set of questions (Appendix B), however when necessary, I asked informants to elaborate on details I thought were important to my study. Our resulting conversation was, thus, somewhat open-ended, which Adkins, drawing on Patton, describes as a way to "be sure that the data [is] comprehensive while still allowing room for discussion and context to shape the results" (26).

I used Nvivo 9 to code and analyze patterns in comments on training evaluations, which were then looked at alongside information presented in the training texts and patterns in tutor interviews. Similar to Ozkan, I chose Nvivo 9 for my analysis because of its capacity to not only code data but also build theories, organize sources, run queries, pull coded segments of data from sources and view those segments collectively, or jump to a particular segment as it appeared in the context of its original source. Manipulating data in this way was very useful in this study, since I was, as Dorothy Smith recommends (29), being careful not to impose any predetermined theory onto the data, but rather looking for the data itself to suggest the kinds of assumptions about literacy that tutors were constructing.[2]

I used the training texts in order to triangulate trainees' comments on training evaluations and tutor interviews. The Basic Literacy training program used two texts: *Tutor* (Colvin), a textbook published nationally by New Reader's Press; and *The Training Manual*, a collection of handouts, a job description, and a list of resources prepared by the training instructors to correspond with each training session.

Limitations

The population size of tutors I interviewed limited me from being able to generalize about tutors' reaction to the training as a result of their prior work and education experience, or as a result of their age, sex, and current profession. It would have been interesting to see, for example, if volunteers who had prior training as teachers were affected differently by the training than someone with no training in education, or to see how the construct of literacy operating in the training affected older and younger volunteers in their experience with the training and in their tutoring practices.

Given the fact that community literacy programs like EAL must serve highly localized populations, with a wide variety of differences (Greenberg 40), and the fact that programs are often restricted in different ways by funding, location, and the kind of presence they can establish in a community, they vary largely in their preferred methods of tutoring and in the ways they train tutors to enact those methods perhaps necessarily. Such a variety makes it difficult to generalize about literacy programs based on the data I've collected.

Findings: Training Texts and Tutoring Strategies

I found three kinds of similarities and divergences among the sets of assumptions tutors, trainees, and the training texts were constructing about literacy and literacy learning. First, I found patterns with regard to the way tutors, trainees, and training texts were defining literacy. Second, I was able to collect findings on the attitudes each took up with regards to planning and preparing for tutoring sessions. Third, I found similarities and differences among the strategies tutors, trainees, and training texts noted in their approach to tutoring.

Definitions of Literacy

Literacy is defined in *Tutor* and *The Training Manual* as a process of sending and receiving information, mediated by *thinking* (Figure 1). The diagram at right is taken from *The Training Manual*. A similar diagram appears in *Tutor*, although the circles around *reading* are not presented in *Tutor*'s version.

In Figure 1, literacy is further broken down as a relationship among four components of language: listening and speaking, associated with receiving information, and reading and writing, associated with expressing information. These components appear to be mediated by thinking, which is, in the diagram, a cognitive function. Listening, reading, speaking, and writing are further categorized in terms of receiving information and expressing information. *Tutor* tells us, "reading, writing listening, speaking—all require the individual to think, to engage in the process of expressing or receiving information" (14). *Tutor* also devotes special attention to reading, although in a different way than *The Training Manual*. Tutor defines reading from the perspective of three "views": "pronouncing words," "identifying and defining words," and "constructing meaning" (Figure 2). *Tutor* tells readers that the first two views of reading, "pronouncing words" and "identifying and defining words" are insufficient at explaining how reading actually happens (18). Although *Tutor* rejects these first two views, they ironically find their way into the diagram, seemingly enshrined in elevated positions above the third view, which *Tutor* adopts as an accurate explanation of reading. The third view defines reading as "bringing meaning to a text in order to understand it" (18). *Tutor* places its third view of reading at the foundation of the pyramid, perhaps suggesting that bringing meaning to a text is the foundation on which reading happens.

Training evaluations from Basic Literacy training included relatively few references to how literacy was defined, when compared to references to other parts of training like lesson planning and tutoring strategies. Out of 264 references to useful

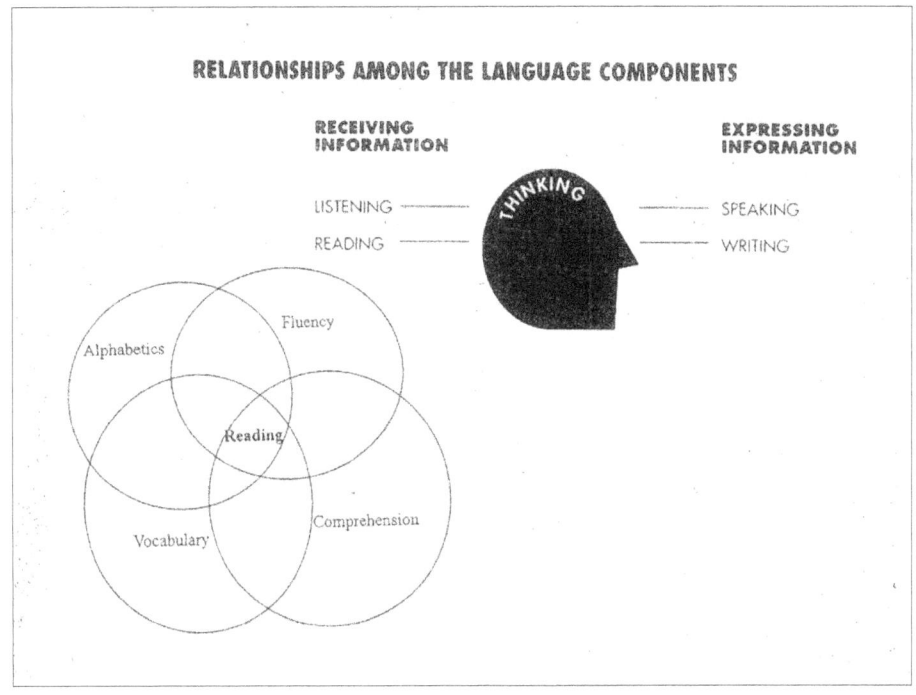

Figure 1. Relationships Among the Language Component. EAL's diagram constructing literacy for the Basic Literacy tutor-training program.

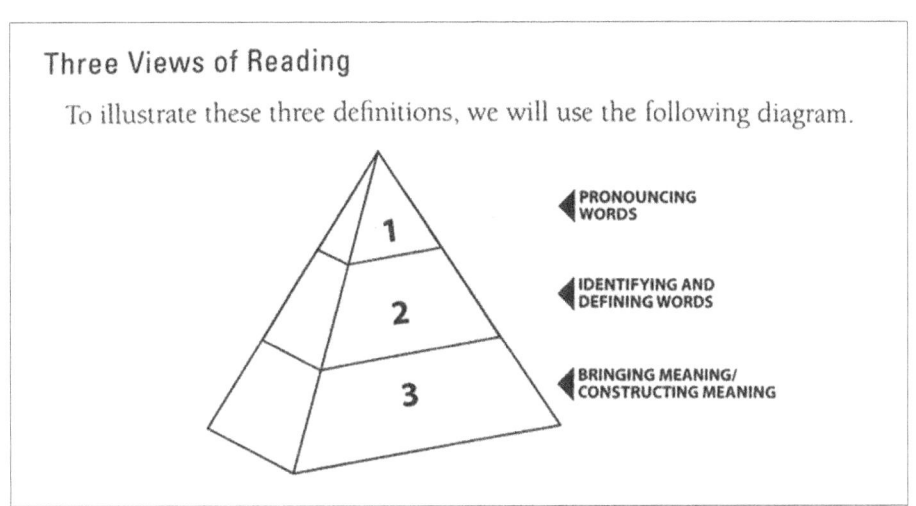

Figure 2. Three Views of Reading. EAL's construct of reading in its Basic Literacy tutor-training program.

aspects of Basic Literacy training, only nine referred to definitions of literacy; and out of eighty-nine references to least useful aspects, only two of those referred to definitions of literacy.

Despite the low number of references to definitions of literacy during the training, all of the tutors I interviewed acknowledged that students do have their own specific literacy goals. These tutors seemed to recognize differences in literacies in relation to different goals. Two tutors, Charlie and Hank, are typical examples of the tutors' disposition to their work:

Charlie:
Whether they want to learn how to
fill out a job application,
or if they just want to be able to read a blueprint, or whatever it is,
I mean that's what you gotta worry about.

Hank:
If they're specifically interested
in getting into a certain school
or taking a certain test.
I say help them.
Why not? It all goes hand in hand.

Although both Charlie and Hank use particular examples of the kinds of things they think a learner might be interested in working on, they both assume any learner-defined goal is what they, as tutors, should be concerned with.

Yet, even though tutors like Charlie and Hank implied that they gave their students authority over their own literacy goals, some others indicated that they were helping their students work toward an all-encompassing literacy. Amy, for example, spoke more directly about "reading ability," which came to mean a kind of universal act of decoding print. Amy was a former high school teacher in the 1970s. Her approach to literacy tutoring as fostering reading ability seemed to correspond with the training texts' definitions of literacy and reading as universal yet student-centered processes.

Amy:
the person you're tutoring needs a lot of praise
for their desire to **increase their reading ability**,
their courage in asking for that assistance,
and just not to give false praise, but to continually look for small gains
and praise, and help that person to see that small gains are very important
to getting at that larger goal they have of **reading more fluently**.

Amy notes a desire to increase her students' "reading ability." In noting this, Amy attributes ownership to students' literacy and distinguishes it from her own. That is, Amy gives the impression that, as a tutor, the literacy she is developing in her students is inherently *theirs*. In addition to making her students owners of their own literacy, Amy also indicates that achieving fluency is part of a "larger goal."

Discussion: Definitions of Literacy

The definition of literacy that EAL adopts in its training program seems to approach literacy as a cognitive phenomenon that occurs when thought mediates the reception and expression of information. More specifically, reading is defined as a process of "bringing meaning" to a text. Both of these can be seen as giving students ownership over their own meaning making abilities. However, residual aspects of literacy as a decontextualized set of reading and writing abilities are also present in these definitions of literacy and reading. In their definition of literacy, thinking is not tied to any social or cultural context. In the three views on reading, word identification, definition, and pronunciation are present in the top two places in the pyramid.

It appears that tutors are able to use this construct to make learners' goals the center of tutoring instruction, though such instruction may also work to marginalize learners' abilities by failing to acknowledge socio-cultural influences on the various ways reading, listening, speaking, and writing occur and for what purposes. Instead, learners' goals may be acknowledged by tutors, but the approaches tutors take to pursue those goals may focus more on the kind of singular, decontextualized reading ability that Amy refers to.

The low number of references to definitions of literacy in the training evaluations may suggest that definitions of literacy were simply not something that trainees considered during training. As we will see in my findings about lesson planning and tutoring strategies, trainees' comments on training evaluations suggests that they were more concerned with what they might do in tutoring sessions, rather than what kinds of assumptions about literacy they might be bringing to their work as a literacy tutor. However, despite the low number of references to definitions of literacy, tutors interviewed seemed to understand the need to let students set their own literacy goals, thus letting their students guide them rather than guiding students toward a preconceived ideal of literacy. For example, Charlie and Hank, like other tutors interviewed, indicate that students' goals should be the focus of literacy instruction. However, Amy's assumptions about literacy seem to include a decontextualized ideal of reading. Amy's references to fluent reading and reading ability seem to represent universal characteristics of reading and writing separated from social and cultural contexts. Following Gee, we might ask in what contexts are fluency and ability measured?

Charlie's and Hank's approach to tutoring as a student-driven endeavor seems to reflect the definition of literacy set forth in *Tutor* and *The Training Manual*. That is, their attitude seems to authorize students' own "thinking" as a mediator of "sending" and "receiving" information. Amy, on the other hand, is inclined to praise students for approaching an ideal reading ability or fluency. This suggests that students may be de-authorized of their way of thinking through encouragement toward an idealized way of thinking.

Lesson Planning

Tutor and the *Training Manual* present two conflicting approaches to lesson planning. The *Training Manual* presents a lesson plan worksheet that includes a predetermined curriculum, while *Tutor*'s approach, though it offers a structure, is open-ended. The lesson plan in *The Training Manual* presents tutors with a numbered outline that describes six portions of a typical lesson and explains the rationale for each portion. Each of these numbers is labeled as a predetermined activity, such as "read aloud," "word study," or having the tutor model writing for the learner (Appendix C). The use of numbered activities in *The Training Manual*'s lesson plan may suggest that lessons should be planned in sequential steps, and that each lesson should include the predetermined activities. In contrast, *Tutor*'s lesson plan presents a list of unnumbered lines. Scattered among the lines are four sections: "Review Previous Lesson," "Activities," "Homework," and "Reading for Pleasure" (Colvin). *Tutor*'s lesson plan does not require tutors to plan lessons in steps as *The Training Manual* does. In addition, the format leaves open space for the tutor and learner to define what to do and how to do it. *Tutor*'s lesson plan also differs from *The Training Manual* by including a space for goals to be defined and comments made by both tutor and learner.

Given the differences between the two training texts' approaches to lesson planning, it is also significant that trainees' comments on training evaluations frequently referenced lesson planning. Out of a total of sixty-one BL and ELL evaluations, tutors made reference to lesson planning on twenty-seven of those evaluations. This means that approximately 50% of training evaluations from both BL and ELL trainings noted lesson planning. Within those references to lesson planning, tutors expressed a desire to know more about lesson planning in ten evaluations. So, approximately one sixth of tutors indicated a desire to know more about lesson planning. Such a high frequency of comments regarding lesson planning suggests that it was an important factor for trainees at EAL.

However, despite its importance for trainees, only two of the eight tutors I interviewed discussed lesson planning in any detail. Interestingly, the two tutors' approaches to lesson planning diverged from each other in the same way as *The Training Manual*'s and *Tutor*'s approaches to lesson planning. The first tutor, Sarah, approached lesson planning in a similar way as the *Training Manual*. Sarah had a background in the hard sciences, and she told me that she felt she was most comfortable in a more rigidly structured work environment. Sarah mentioned that she previously volunteered for a different organization where she was accustomed to taking direction from a supervisor and negotiating her volunteer work with others during weekly meetings. Sarah indicated that she was reassured by her lesson planning strategy, which followed a predetermined set of steps, similar to *The Training Manual*'s approach to lesson planning.

Sarah:
>The training I had was good.
>The two that stick the most with me that were the most helpful
>was when there was an actual teacher.
>She used to be a special ed teacher,
>but she no longer was,
>but she said, "I don't have time for lesson plans.
>I go to Borders and I buy a book.
>I follow the book."
>She was very reassuring.

Sarah later revealed that the book she used was called *The Wilson Reading System*. According to Wilson Language Training website, the Wilson Reading System "directly teaches the structure of words in the English language with an organized and sequential system with twelve steps. Steps 1 and 2 emphasize phonemic segmentation skills (the ability to separate the sounds in a word) and blending the sounds together again" (Wilson Reading System). Sarah said that her choice to use *The Wilson Reading System* to plan her lessons grew out of the special education teacher's encouragement that lesson planning was not necessary for literacy tutoring. She also told me that the special education teacher was, in fact, one of the BL training instructors at EAL.

Charlie was the other tutor who referenced lesson planning in his interview. Charlie revealed that he had previously worked as a fireman, and that the crews he worked with were the reason he decided to become a volunteer literacy tutor. He described an approach to lesson planning that seemed to aligned somewhat with *Tutor* in that Charlie left lessons open-ended. However, unlike the approach to planning set forth in *Tutor,* Charlie's approach may have differed, given his emphasis on leaving lessons unplanned.

Charlie:
> you can't go in with a set plan,
> you can't go in with a lesson plan,
> you just go in, and you do what they need.
> […]
> That I kind of just kind of do whatever,
> like I say I don't concentrate on lesson plans, I don't.
> and I think with the clientele that I get:
> the more informal,
> the more relaxed,
> the better off you are with these guys.
> And I would stress that more in the training, than what they do.

Charlie's improvisational approach grew out of his perception of his students and the kind of disposition he felt they had toward literacy education. Throughout the interview he implied that planning creates a tenser dynamic between him and the person he works with.

Discussion: Attitudes Toward Lesson Planning

I draw on these examples to show that Charlie and Sarah were not in fact confused about lesson planning; rather I want to illustrate the variety of lesson planning approaches that resulted from their completion of the same BL training program. Both Charlie and Sarah adopted two different approaches to lesson planning. Charlie's approach was more open-ended, since he did not concentrate on lesson plans. Sarah's was more regimented, as she adopted a step-by-step approach that involved predetermined activities from the *Wilson Reading System*.

However, neither Charlie nor Sarah used the specific lesson plan forms available in *Tutor* or the *Training Manual*. Their approaches were adapted after they completed the training and began tutoring. This suggests that the habits they developed as tutors resulted not from the training but from the actual tutoring itself. Given their backgrounds, their approach might also support suggestions made by Ceprano and Talarr—that volunteers' backgrounds tend to be a significant influence on the tutoring strategies they develop. Since they began tutoring after the training program ended, the training did not have control over the habits that Charlie and Sarah were developing. The fact that the lesson planning habits that Charlie and Sarah took up were divergent from each other might correspond with the BL training's own inconsistent constructions of lesson planning. Charlie's and Sarah's development of divergent approaches after completing the training could support Belzer's claim that "a few broad and important ideas", such as an open-ended or a regimented approach to planning, tend to transfer from training to tutoring, whereas the specific techniques, such as the use of particular lesson planning forms, may not (135).

Tutoring Strategies for Developing Comprehension

Tutor defines comprehension as "the accurate understanding of what is read" (71). Using "the" to present "accurate understanding" seems to suggest that there is only one possible understanding of what is read. Likewise, tutoring strategies that focus on "the accurate understanding" seem to offer only one correct or incorrect answer. These strategies de-contextualize language by divorcing language from the role it plays in a particular text and social context. For example, teaching grammar rules, single word recognition, and phonics presents words and rules of language as separate from their function in a particular text. One printout in *The Training Manual* titled "Spelling Practice" describes steps for memorizing a single word, and the goal of "Spelling Practice" is to develop the ability to spell multiple de-contextualized words. Likewise, in *Tutor*, strategies such as "Phonics: Letter-Sounds Relationships" and "Word Patterns," rely on de-contextualized language. In *Tutor*, "Phonics" strategies involved recognizing the sound of individual letters and then identifying those sounds in letters of individual words. "Word Patterns" strategies involve writing a list of words that rhyme, such as cap, map, and lap, repeating the words, and sounding out the letters in each word (Colvin).

The Training Manual adopts a different definition of comprehension. It suggests that the goal of teaching comprehension is to "help student[s] learn to monitor their own thinking while reading." That is, *The Training Manual* defines comprehension as being self-aware of one's own thoughts. One strategy that enacts this definition is the "think aloud." *The Training Manual* defines "think aloud" as a "comprehension activity" that asks learners to read a passage and say out loud what they are thinking as they read. According to the exercise, some examples of thinking out loud include: making predictions about what the text will be about, coping with difficulties in the text, describing images, and describing how prior knowledge links to an understanding of the text. After the learner thinks aloud, the exercise asks the tutor to "discuss with the student(s) the kind of thinking you did while reading. Does he/she think that similar strategies would help him/her with comprehension?" (*The Training Manual* 10). Through this strategy, it appears that readers' various interpretations are recognized insofar as those interpretations are thought aloud by the reader. The purpose is not to find a single accurate meaning; rather it is to understand how a reader is constructing any particular meaning.

Out of all the evaluation comments specifically referencing tutor training, references concerning tutoring strategies were the most frequent (Table 1). The second most frequent were references to specific content covered in the training. I distinguished references to "content" from references to "tutoring strategies" by noting where trainees were simply made note of an idea that occurred during training as opposed to places where trainees mentioned something from the training that they felt could be practically applied to their tutoring. I identified any mention of practically applying some idea, method, approach, or tactics as "tutoring strategies." The high frequency of references among trainees to tutoring strategies indicates that strategies that can be applied to tutoring are important to trainees.

Table 1: Aspects of Tutor Training Referenced in Evaluation Comments

	Total n	Tutoring Strategies	Content of Training	Questions about tutoring	Lesson planning	The use of resources
References	761	279 (36%)	124 (16%)	107 (14%)	68 (9%)	61 (8%)
Sources	65	44 (67%)	44 (67%)	41 (63%)	27 (41%)	28 (43%)

I found that the most highly referenced categories of strategies tended to refer to generalized strategies like "planning a lesson" or "working with a student," rather than specific strategies like the "think aloud," or "spelling practice," which were just two of many presented in the training texts. In fact, the least-referenced strategies tended to be the more specific ones. For example, "how to do a read aloud" was only referenced three times, compared to "ideas to use when tutoring," which was referenced 39 times (Table 2). These less frequently referenced strategies identified a particular goal or activity, whereas the highly referenced strategies referred more generally to issues that relate to tutoring, such as planning a lesson or working with a learner without recognizing planning a lesson for a *particular* purpose, or working with a learner to accomplish a *particular* goal.

Table 2: Evaluation References to Strategies Applicable to Tutoring

	Total n	How to plan a lesson	Ideas to use when tutoring	How to work with a student	How to do a read aloud	Pronunciation techniques
References	267	39	39	19	3	2
Sources	43	23	24	14	2	2

Also, four tutors interviewed indicated that they took up tutoring strategies generally. For example, when I asked Rebecca what strategies she would recommend to new tutors, she pointed out that recommending specific strategies would be difficult, since each tutor-learner pair presents different challenges.

Ryan:
>If you were to be met with a tutor that's just completing the training program, what sort of advice or strategies would you recommend to them in the tutoring?

Rebecca:
>You know that's hard to say because, uh,
>I think there's different types of tutoring that you do.
>And I think as a student,
>and I think the other students feel the same way,
>we almost wish we would have known
>what our tutoring assignment was gonna be
>when we took the course.

When I asked Kathy a similar question about tutoring strategies, she also did not mention any particular strategies that a new tutor might use. Instead, Kathy described the resources that tutors might seek out to discover their own strategies.

Ryan:
>If you had to recommend tutoring strategies
>to a tutor that's just starting,
>what tutoring strategies would you recommend
>to someone just beginning
>or what advice would you give?

Kathy:
>Ok, you said volunteer
>[…] There are many resources offered by [EAL].
>Including on the committee there are other tutors
>who are willing to help you
>every time you get a little nervous or, you know,
>run out of your own ideas.
>So that's one, the resources are there.
>You know all kinds of materials to help.
>And, I personally love researching the internet.

For Kathy, it seems, tutoring strategies are something she developed while tutoring, by looking for answers on the Internet or in the resources EAL makes available to each tutor.

Discussion: Composing Strategies

General adoption of tutoring strategies, such as focusing on "lesson planning" and "working with a learner," may be the result of trainees not knowing who their tutor-learner match is. The fact that more general strategies tended to be referenced much more frequently than specific strategies might point to trainees' uncertainty about how these strategies might be useful in specific tutoring situations. That is to say, trainees were learning about tutoring strategies without having the experience of tutoring., nor did trainees know whom they would be working with. Therefore, tutoring strategies introduced during training must have been conceptualized in hypothetical situations, such as planning for a lesson, working with a learner, or just generally tutoring. So when I claim that trainees could have been uncertain about how strategies would be useful, I am saying that without active tutoring experience, trainees might not have developed a sense of how these strategies would actually work in specific situations. Thus, they more often noted general strategies about working with a learner, and not a strategy for conducting a read aloud.

Allowing tutors to discover their own strategies is perhaps more useful than recommending strategies because of the challenges presented by the variety of tutoring situations, as Rebecca points out. As Greenberg reminds us, adult learners approach literacy organizations with a wide variety of goals (40), which in turn could challenge tutors to adapt strategies to unique situations. Because of this challenge, EAL's Basic Literacy tutor training may be more effective if tutors are taught how to search and adapt strategies to their own unique tutoring situations, rather than presenting predetermined strategies to be understood in an abstract sense, divorced from any actual tutoring. The same claim could be made for lesson planning. If trainees are matched with a particular learner while in the process of being trained in techniques of lesson planning, then trainees might be in a better position to adapt lesson planning techniques around the goals and interests of their learner, instead of conceptualizing lesson planning in an abstract sense around hypothetical goals and interests.

Conclusions

As volunteer tutors move through the training program and eventually onto tutoring, they are involved in a process of becoming "literate" in the practices of student-centered adult literacy tutoring. As Talarr suggests, the training process should aim to move volunteers into the habits and values of the institution in which participants are being trained (385). In the case of EAL, it seems that tutors were developing most of their tutoring practices after completing the training and as they were active in tutoring their students. A similar process of developing skills through participating in the work is reflected in Berkenkotter et al. who observe "Nate's" identity as a writer as it develops within and against the activity of Carnegie Mellon's Rhetoric Program (39-40). If we consider that tutors are still training themselves as they face their specific tutoring contexts, it's not surprising that tutors demonstrated a wide variety of approaches to lesson planning and "comprehension" strategies. Volunteers bring their own experiences to bear on their tutoring practices, and using those experiences, rather than training knowledge and resources, adapt their tutoring to specific students, and such students, as Greenberg mentions, also vary widely in their backgrounds, goals, and purposes.

During the time of this study, EAL's Basic Literacy tutor-training program was operating with two separate, and perhaps conflicting constructs of literacy, as evidenced by the program's definition of literacy. On one hand, literacy meant a cognitively situated reception and expression of information, which recognized literacies as multiple and grounded in the way an individual interacts with a text—a construct that positions reading and writing as contextual. However, the program's definition of reading as also "pronouncing words," and "defining words" constructs literacy as a set of abilities that can be learned once and for all and applied regardless of the contexts or purposes in which they are used.

Given these assumptions about literacy, I also asked how such an approach to literacy tutoring affects the tutoring practices of volunteer literacy tutors who complete the training. Similar to their definitions of literacy, the training texts used to train BL tutors at EAL seem to implement tutoring strategies that construct literacy as detached from social contexts, thus inhibiting instructors from considering possibilities of matching trainees with tutors as part of the training. Basic Literacy training assumes varying definitions of comprehension. On one hand, strategies like "think aloud" and "The Language Approach" align themselves with a definition of comprehension that recognizes the validity of multiple possible interpretations of a text. The "think aloud" strategy is particularly unique, since it not only recognizes multiple possible interpretations of a text, but it also works to make readers aware of the interpretations they are making. On the other hand, many more strategies promote teaching de-contextualized language, which is aligned with the definition of comprehension as "the accurate understanding of what is read" (*Tutor*).

Based on my interviews with tutors, it seems that there is a felt sense that practical experience would in fact be a valuable part of adult literacy tutor training. Such a felt sense aligns with current understanding of literacy as a socially situated activity (as described by Gee; Russell; Prior & Shipka). In addition, Russell tells us that for newcomers, any new ways of acting or thinking are developed through continued interaction with others already habituated in those ways of acting or thinking (516). Newcomers to adult literacy tutoring—e.g. trainees—seem to begin developing conceptual grounding of student-centered tutoring in training; however, translating that knowledge to one-on-one tutoring situations seems altogether different than learning about it in a classroom. This study supports the argument that trainees' notions of student-centered literacy tutoring remain incomplete without the actual experience of tutoring.

If, as Rebecca recommended, trainees are matched with learners as part of the training rather than as a result, then the conflicting constructs of literacy tutoring set forth by *Tutor* and *The Training Manual* might serve as fruitful sites of learning, since trainees could experience the effect that varying constructs of literacy have on the social contexts of literacy tutoring. This recommendation is in support of D'Amico & Schnee who argue that "political bureaucratic, cultural [...] and economic factors that govern access to jobs" play a significant part in adult literacy learning (136). D'Amico and Schnee argue that tutor training should prepare tutors to address the socio-cultural factors that are not reading and writing practices in themselves, but nevertheless influence how those practices are used in a particular social context. Such learning could occur as tutors bring their experience of tutoring into contact with the approaches to lesson planning and teaching strategies set forth by the two training texts. For example, a trainee who plans a lesson, meets with his or her learner, enacts particular tutoring strategies, and then attends a training session on lesson planning would be in a better position to critically examine concepts of lesson planning conducted in the training because that trainee has had the experience of testing those concepts in a real-life environment.

Appendix A

Figure A1. Institutional Structure of Eastern Adult Literacy's Basic Literacy Training

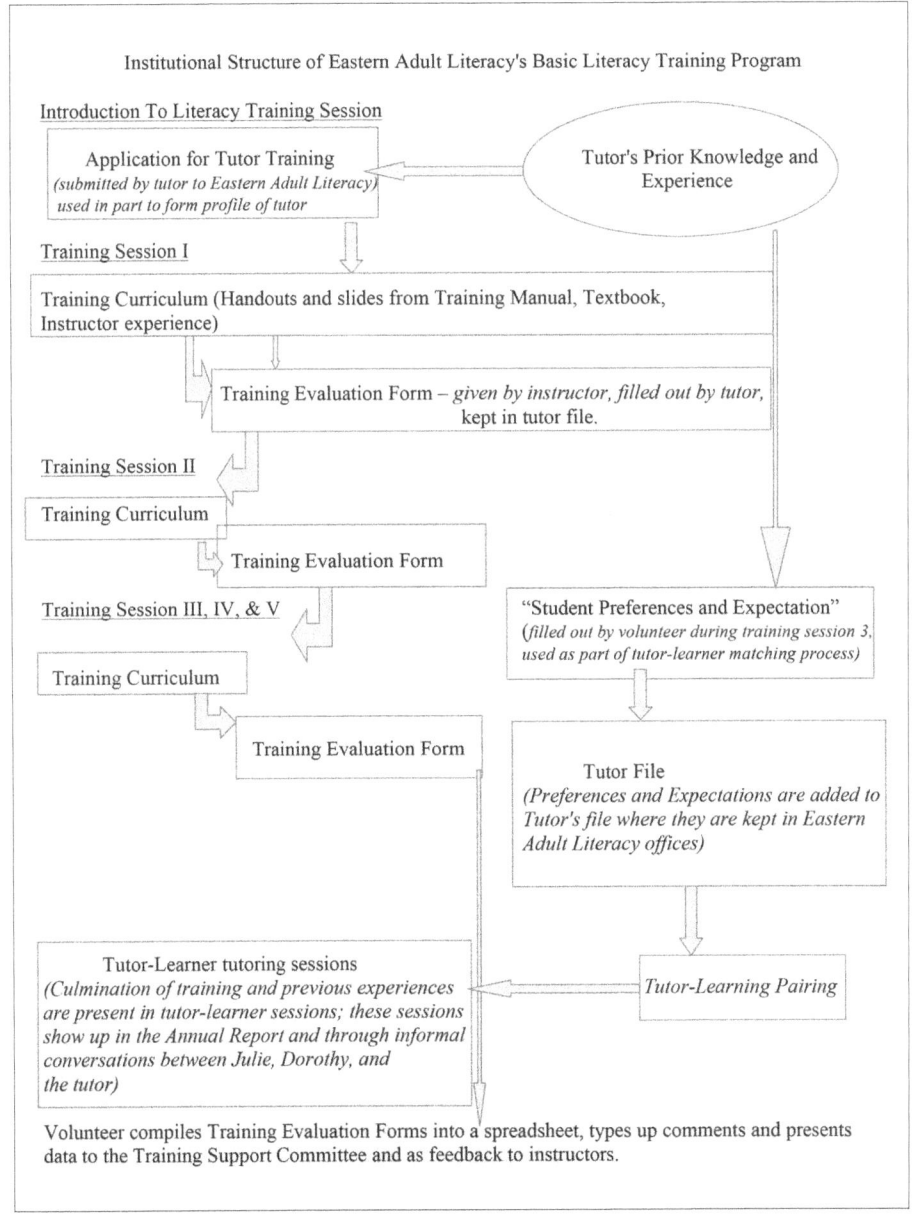

Appendix B

Interview Protocol used to Interview Tutors

Interview Schedule for Tutors
How long have you been a tutor?
1. What brought you to tutoring with [EAL]?
2. What tutoring strategies for tutoring would you recommend to a tutor who is just starting out?
3. What might you caution a beginning tutor against doing?
4. Can you talk a little about your experience with the tutor training program?
5. What, if anything, might you add to or change about the training process?
6. Is there anything specific from your training experience that you feel has made its way into your tutoring?
7. What was your experience like being paired up with a student?
8. Is there anything else you'd like to say about adult literacy tutoring in general?

Appendix C

The Training Manual's Lesson Planning Worksheet

TYPICAL LESSON TEMPLATE

The following outline provides a list of suggested components for a typical lesson. These suggestions should be used after the student/tutor relationship has been established. See Tutor, p.176-77, for additional information about planning for lessons.

1. Read aloud (10 – 15 min. at beginning of lesson)

 Book Title: _____

2. Review reading and/or assignments from previous session (10 min.)

 _____

3. Student reads aloud to tutor (10 - 15 min.)

 Selection: _____

4. Word Study (10 - 15 min.)

 Activity: _____

5. Student writes with tutor (15 min.)

 Selection: _____

6. Introduce new books or chapters to student; assign work for next session; set goals.
 (5 – 10 min.)

 Book or chapter title for pleasure reading: _____

 Assignment: _____

 Goals: _____

Session II   Page 22   Revised 1.2010

Appendix D

Tutor's Lesson Planning Worksheet

LESSON PLAN

Student's name: _____ Lesson #: _____ Lesson date: _____
Tutor's name: _____ Length of lesson: _____
Lesson goal/objectives _____
_____

Review homework _____
_____

	This session	Next session
Review previous lesson		
New work or work in progress		
Activities		
Homework		
Reading for pleasure		
Student comments		
Tutor notes		

APPENDIX · TUTOR, 8TH EDITION

End Notes

1. Names of organizations and participants in this article are pseudonyms.
2. My data analysis took on two phases. In the first phase of coding, I created nodes to label patterns in the data that looked to be recurring themes, or simply interesting in some way. I coded training evaluations and interview transcripts separately. Dealing with training evaluations first and then interview transcripts allowed me to distinguish patterns in training evaluations from those in the interview transcripts. This separation was made, because I did not want a close look at the tutors' interviews to inadvertently influence how I was reading evaluation comments. I coded evaluation comments under categories that represented the four questions asked of trainees: (1) "what was the most useful information presented?" (2) "what was the least useful information presented?" (3) "are you prepared to tutor?" and (4) "what other questions do you have?" After this general coding procedure, I looked for patterns under each category of question. For interview transcripts, I created nodes for each question I asked in my interview protocol. Then, I focused on one question across multiple informants. As I looked specifically at multiple informants' responses to the same question, I then created nodes to label those patterns as I did for the training evaluations.

In the second phase of coding, I analyzed the nodes that had been created from both evaluation comments and interview transcripts in order to identify similarities and divergences across the range of nodes I had identified. For example, in many cases, several separate nodes were compiled under a common label. That is, in one case I noticed that references to meeting the needs of learners, recognizing small gains, and modeling active learning were all constructing a tutor's role in a one-on-one tutoring situation. "Tutor's Role" then became a parent node under which nodes describing the tutor's role were sorted. Sorting the nodes in this way allowed me to identify what tutors and trainees were talking about most often and how many tutors and trainees were talking about the same things.

In addition to using Nvivo 9 to analyze interview transcripts and training evaluations, I conducted a close reading of the training texts, *Tutor* and *The Training Manual*, in order to draw connections among interviews and evaluations. I was not able to analyze the training texts in Nvivo 9, since I did not have electronic copies, and scanning the pages individually into Nvivo proved to be too time-consuming. In order to supplement my reading of the training texts, I drew on my notes from training observations. These notes helped guide me to sections of the training texts that seemed to be holding more importance for tutors and trainees.

Works Cited

Adkins, Tabetha. "The English Effect" on Amish Language and Literacy Practices." *Community Literacy Journal*, 5.2 (2011): 39-54.

Belzer, Aliza. "Less May be More: Rethinking Adult Literacy Volunteer Tutor Training." *Journal of Literacy Research.* 38 (2006): 111-140.

Berkenkotter, Carol, Thomas N. Huckin, and John Ackerman. "Conventions, Conversations and the Writer: Case Study of a Student in a Rhetoric Ph.D. Program. *Research in the Teaching of English.* 22.1 (1988): 9-44.

Cheville, Julie, and Margaret Finders. "Defining Adolescent and Adult Writing Development: A Contest of Empirical and Federal Wills." *Handbook of Research on Writing*. Eds. Charles Bazerman et al. New York: Lawrence Erlbaum Associates, 2008. 421-433

Colvin, Ruth. *Tutor: A Collaborative, Learner-centered Approach to Literacy Instruction for Teens and Adults*. 8th ed. Syracuse, NY: New Readers Press, 2009.

D'Amico, Debby, and Emily Schnee. "It Changed Something Inside of Me: English Language Learning, Structural Barriers to Employment, and Workers' Goals in a Workplace Literacy Program. *Changing Work, Changing Workers: Critical Perspectives on Language, Literacy, and Skills*. Ed. G. Hull New York: SUNY, 1997. 117-140.

Eastern Adult Literacy. "How Can You Volunteer?" *Eastern Adult Literacy Website*. Retrieved Feb. 2012.

_____. *Training Manual*. Eds. EAL Staff and Instructors. 2011.

Freire, Paolo. *Pedagogy of the Oppressed*. New York: Continuum, 1993.

Gee, James. "Literacy and 'Traditions.'" *Journal of Education*, 17.1 (1989): 26-38.

Godbee, Beth "Resisting Altruism: How Systematic Power and Privilege Become Personal in One-on-one Community Tutoring." *Community Literacy Journal*, 3.2 (2009): 37-52.

Greenberg, Daphne. "The challenges facing adult literacy programs." *Community Literacy Journal*. 3.1 (2008): 39-54.

Ozkan, Betul C. "Using NVivo to Analyze Qualitative Classroom Data on Constructivist Learning Environments." *The Qualitative Report*. 9.4 (2004): 589-603.

Patton, Michael Quinn. *Qualitative Research and Evaluation Methods*. 3rd ed. Thousand Oaks, CA: Sage, 2002.

Pomerance, Anita. *Volunteers tutoring adults: The construction of literacy by tutor-student pairs*. University of Pennsylvania. Unpublished dissertation, 1990.

Prior, Paul, and Jody Shipka,. "Chronotopic lamination: tracing the contours of literate activity. *Writing Selves/Writing Societies*. Eds. Charles Bazerman and David Russell. 2003. Fort Collins, CO: WAC Clearinghouse. 180-239.

Purcell-Gates, Victoria et al. "Impact of Authentic Adult Literacy Instruction on Adult Literacy Practices." *Reading Research Quarterly*, 37.1 (2002): 70-92.

Russell, David. "Rethinking Genre in School and Society: An Activity Theory Analysis." *Written Communication*, 14.4 (1997): 504-554.

Smith, Dorothy. *Institutional Ethnography: A Sociology for People*. New York: Rowman & Littlefield, 2005.

Smith, Thomas. "The Narrowing of Knowing: What it Means to be Literate and Learned in Today's Society." *Journal of Inquiry and Action in Education*. 1.2 (2008): 35-57.

Smith, Dorothy and Catherine Schryer. "On Documentary Society." *Handbook of Research on Writing*. New York: Lawrence Erlbaum Associates, 2008. 113-127

Street, Brian V. "Recent Applications of New Literacy Studies in Educational Contexts." *Research in the Teaching of English*. 39.4 (2005): 417-423.

Talarr, Carolyn. "Active Listening: A Framework for Introducing Volunteer Tutors to Student-centered Learning." *Journal of Reading*, 38.5 (1995): 384-385.

"Wilson Reading System." *Wilson language training*. Retrieved February 2012. <http://www.wilsonlanguage.com/fs_program_wrs.htm>.

Ryan Roderick is a writing instructor and Graduate Teaching Assistant mentor at University of Maine, Orono.

community literacy journal

A Place for Ecopedagogy in Community Literacy
Rhonda Davis

> *"To speak, people must first listen to what the world has to say."*
> —Judith Halden-Sullivan, *"The Phenomenology of Process"*

Educators focused on community literacy and public engagement have access to a unique critical platform from which larger social issues that impact us both as a whole and on very personal levels are open to exploration. Being particularly situated to have significant impact on community, literacy work in this area may require uncommon pedagogical strategies. Based on its comprehensive focus on sustainability, ecological literacy, sociopolitical factors that affect communities, and a multitude of other factors that underpin social injustice, ecopedagogy may be uniquely positioned to offer a more holistic view than other composition pedagogies such as place-based education and ecocomposition.

In considering the powerful impact writing can have in both the personal and social arenas as a primary mode of communication and expression, we can clearly identify the importance of composition studies. Educators in composition studies, particularly those focused on community literacy and public engagement, have access to a unique critical platform from which larger social issues that impact us both as a whole and on very personal levels are open to exploration. Being uniquely situated to have significant impact on community, literacy work in this area may require unique pedagogical strategies. In light of this, what follows is a discussion of the approach to ecopedagogy as it might apply to community literacy. Based on its comprehensive focus on sustainability, ecological literacy, sociopolitical factors that affect communities, and a multitude of other factors that underpin social injustice, ecopedagogy may offer a more holistic view than other composition pedagogies, such as place-based education and ecocomposition. As ecopedagogy explores the ways in which literacy impacts community needs, it may prove successful in guiding practitioners and participants toward viable solutions for their communities.

This essay, in part, reviews a project discussed by Robert Brooke in "Voices of Young Citizens: Rural Citizenship, Schools, and Public Policy" as a supportive example of how ecopedagogical thinking might be applied to real community literacy concerns. Involving five rural schools in Nebraska with the primary objective of helping rural youth create their own rhetorical space to address community issues, this particular project not only highlights the importance of community literacy efforts but also its unique applicability and possibility within rural settings.

In addition to considering ways in which ecopedagogy might contribute to community literacy, I will discuss an analysis of how ecopedagogy can be utilized in conjunction with the rhetorical model that Lorraine Higgins, Elenore Long, and Linda Flower propose in "Community Literacy: A Rhetorical Model for Personal and Public Inquiry." This model will serve as a framework for both understanding and meeting the challenges of community literacy projects in a rural setting.

Higgins, Long, and Flower claim that "literacy should be defined not merely as the receptive skill of reading, but as the public act of writing and taking social action" (167). The authors define their approach to community literacy as one that "uses writing to support collaborative inquiry into community problems; calls up local publics around the aims of democratic deliberation; and transforms personal and public knowledge by restructuring deliberative dialogues among individuals and groups across lines of difference" (168). Combine this approach to community literacy with the broader ecological scope of ecopedagogy, and practitioners do indeed have a potentially powerful strategy for making real and lasting personal and public change.

Ecopedagogy, evolving from critical pedagogy and pulling from various educational ideas and practices, serves to elevate the mission of composition pedagogy while providing a framework from which practitioners might gain a broader scope to understand the diverse influences communities are subject to. It is widely accepted that the primary mission of ecopedagogy is to guide teachers and practitioners of all types to not only see the collective potential of human beings, but to develop an appreciation for it and to foster social justice. Ecopedagogy also seeks to value local knowledge as well as expert knowledge. In tackling literacy issues that underpin social injustice, ecopedagogy also seeks to embrace the inherently ecological nature of human life and society that requires input from local populations, established experts, and the larger society (Kahn 18). In doing so, it places ecoliteracy at its center and opposes the globalization of ideologies such as neoliberalism and imperialism that may hinder local literacy efforts. Ecopedagogy may be a more comprehensive strategy than those of traditional literacy approaches when working within the field of community literacy as, according to Richard Kahn in *Critical Pedagogy, Ecoliteracy, and Planetary Crisis*, it seeks to humanize experience based on ecologically oriented politics and make connections between culturally relevant forms of knowledge (18).

Other scholars are making the connections between what is defined as culturally relevant knowledge, politics, sustainability, and ecology. Gregory Martin, in "The Poverty of Critical Pedagogy: Toward a Politics of Engagement," claims there is a much needed "revolutionary critical pedagogy based in hope that can bridge the politics of the academy with forms of grassroots political organizing capable of achieving social and ecological transformation" (349). For ecopedagogy, the ideas of planetarity and biophilia must be added to Martin's notion of revolutionary critical pedagogy; we must necessarily approach education, specifically literacy skills, with the underpinning that we are all indeed part of life on earth. As Antonia Darder notes in the preface to Richard Kahn's *Critical Pedagogy, Ecoliteracy, and Planetary Crisis*:

> Any anti-hegemonic resistance movement that claims social justice, universal human rights, or global peace must contend forthrightly with the deteriorating ecological crisis at hand, as well as consider possible strat-

egies and relationships that rupture the status quo and transform environmental conditions that threaten disaster. A failure to integrate ecological sustainability at the core of our political and pedagogical struggles for liberation, Kahn argues, is to blindly and misguidedly adhere to an anthropocentric worldview in which emancipatory dreams are deemed solely about human interests, without attention either to the health of the planet or to the well-being of all species with whom we walk the earth. (xiii)

In adopting ecopedagogy at the outset of community literacy projects, we acknowledge that the health and survival of our communities is dependent upon planetary sustainability and as such, is a "vital and necessary critical pedagogical concern" (Kahn xiii).

In support of these critical pedagogical concerns, what follows is an investigation into the links between community literacy and ecopedagogy. I begin with a brief exploration of the role composition pedagogy and literacy skills play in public engagement and social action. Next, I explore how literacy as an ecological act delves into the ways compositionists and community literacy practitioners see themselves in relation to the world and the positive potential of holding such a view. A discussion of various pedagogical strategies that take into account ecological relationships between writers and their environments follows, claiming that a unique approach to community literacy is warranted. Finally, I detail how ecopedagogy may serve as a powerful and comprehensive approach in community literacy, leading into an analysis of why this may work well in rural literacy programs specifically.

Public Engagement and Social Action

In her essay "Service Learning as the New English Studies," Ellen Cushman notes that "[r]ather than simply imparting literacy skills that are indeed useful in the workplace, much research in rhetoric and composition engages students in the critique and appropriation of literacy practices necessary to influence and change workplaces and communities from within" (205). Both the academic and public spheres appear to be crawling away from strict conceptions of selfhood to constructs that include the wider environments within which we exist. As an additional layer in the unique position educators in composition studies find themselves, we can also examine this broadening of the concept of selfhood and how its more inclusive perspective affects pedagogies and strategies aimed at community literacy.

While the concept of selfhood is expanding, scholars like Christian Weisser argue that the inclusion of the larger biosphere we live in has had little impact on composition theory. In "Ecocomposition and the Greening of Identity," Weisser observes: "In order for composition theory to fully account for the many ways in which human subjectivity is constructed, we must begin to recognize that our own personal, social, and political lives are wholly dependent upon the biological matrix of life on this planet" (82). In doing so, we begin to recognize our own "green identities" and this "moves us closer toward realizing exactly who we are in relation to the rest of the world" (82). What are the consequences of reaching literacy goals for composition studies and community literacy practitioners in particular?

Realizing who we are in relation to the rest of the world as writers and educators is important because writing "can be seen as a search for identity" (Weisser 85). In seeing ourselves as constructing and being constructed *by* the world around us, understanding our relationship to the world is crucial and is undoubtedly expressed in our literacy skills. This fuller understanding of who we are can have tremendous implications for shared problem solving and solution building. In community literacy efforts, community building, identifying shared concerns, giving voice to those concerns, and finding appropriate, fair, and just solutions are all founded on a broader understanding of who we are in relation to the world around us. Weisser asserts that a fuller understanding of our identity in relation to the world will necessitate that "compositionists in particular begin to move toward a more ecological understanding of identity" (87).

Literacy as an Ecological Act

In analyzing literacy practices in terms of affecting a broader scope and set of environments, most noticeably our workplaces and our communities, what we are adopting can be viewed as a more ecological way of looking at the world. We are part of a greater whole—an interdependent network of actions and consequences. Therefore, our discourse ought to reflect the primacy of such a relationship. In "Ecocomposition, Theoretical and Pedagogical Approaches," Sydney Dobrin supports this notion of writing as an ecological act, as we cannot be separated from our environments as we write and are written. He claims that "rhetoric and composition is an ecological endeavor in that writing cannot be separated from place, from environment, from nature, or from location" (13). Dobrin also emphasizes that composition and rhetoric studies is "a study of relationships: between individual writers and their surrounding environments, between writers and texts, between texts and culture, between ideology and discourse, and between language and the world" (12). Nowhere is this more apparent than in community literacy where compositionists take part in analyzing and learning from a matrix of ever-evolving relationships people find themselves, for better or worse, embedded within.

It is critical in this ecological framework to recognize that "identity emerges not only from our human relationships, but from the connections we have with other lifeforms in an array of habitats" (Weisser 87). While ecological literacy and the pedagogical approaches that result do not focus exclusively on environmental concerns, they have the potential to expand participants' awareness of such concerns. Once one's identity is expanded to include other life forms and environments, a more ecological imagining of our relationship with the world we live in becomes more evident. An ecological framework opens up understanding and appreciation for the biodiversity of which we are a part, and the need for preservation of such diversity becomes apparent.

As citizens, students, teachers, and writers, we are embedded within particular environments that affect us, engage us, and challenge us. It is a reciprocal relationship that involves other people, nonhuman others, the natural environment, and constructed environments. In order to effect socially responsible change, which many composition scholars believe to be an integral goal of teaching, it is critical to embrace this ecological concept in teaching composition and rhetoric, as well as to engage in public discourse. Writing is a fundamentally human activity, and when viewed from an ecological stance, it cannot be separated from human experience.

A Unique Pedagogical Requirement

As an ecological act, literacy holds tremendous potential for real civic engagement and tangible social change. When one views oneself in terms of being an active part of an interdependent whole, a dynamic, integrated way of thinking must take hold, one that forces a larger world view and therefore specific approaches to being in the world. As a composition instructor, course design and implementation would necessarily be geared with this in mind—aiding and guiding the student in the formation of a more ecologically minded approach to optimally meeting personal and social challenges. The same holds true for community literacy practitioners; program design and practical application of an ecological approach incorporate the multifaceted aspects of a community's identity.

Scholars like Ellen Cushman and Thomas Deans also support this notion that an integral goal of teaching is to effect socially responsible change and that helping students develop a critical consciousness to that end is essential. If, as Thomas Deans asserts, an "important goal of composition courses is to encourage critical consciousness" and that our objective as teachers is to help our students "to see problems as systemic" and "to see things from multiple perspectives," then an ecological approach is inevitable (99).

The ecological approach to composition and rhetoric has not been fully explored when it comes to applicability both inside and outside the classroom. In community literacy, its potential becomes even more visible as students and community members may begin to see their writing and their participation in community literacy as not only an important part of our democracy but as a liberating personal action. Clearly, a unique pedagogical approach is needed for such a powerful and engaging framework.

An approach that is gaining ground in both public education and community literacy programs is *place-based education*. Scholars in the field of place-based education agree that centering on local issues, both cultural and geographical, serves more long-term good than a more "migratory" approach as discussed by Robert Brooke. David Sobel, author of *Childhood and Nature, Design Principles for Educators* and *Place-Based Education, Connecting Classrooms & Communities*, has done much to advance the pedagogy and provide teachers and other educators with the tools to fully embrace place-based education. Sobel defines place-based education as

> the process of using the local community and environment as a starting point to teach concepts in language arts, mathematics, social studies, science, and other subject areas across the curriculum. Emphasizing hands-on, real-world learning experiences, this approach to education increases academic achievement, helps students develop stronger ties to their com-

munity, enhances students' appreciation for the natural world, and creates a heightened commitment to serving as active, contributing citizens. Community vitality and environmental quality are improved through the active engagement of local citizens, community organizations, and environmental resources in the life of the school. (164)

According to Sobel in *Place-Based Education: Connecting Classrooms & Communities*, place-based education is "not solely a way to integrate the curriculum around a study of place, but a means of inspiring stewardship and an authentic renewal and revitalization of civic life," (iii) and as such, cannot focus only on local realities. No community exists within a cultural, economic, or political vacuum. Communities are shaped by these forces and as such, guide students to take part in the larger world to which they belong.

While making connections between the larger culture and local realities, is place-based composition only a starting point for community literacy? In "Deep Maps, Teaching Rhetorical Engagement through Place-Conscious Education," Robert Brooke and Jason McIntosh introduce the notion of using maps to both represent and connect with the places we find ourselves—both literal and abstract. Two main objectives in using deep maps are that they help develop considered space and encourage civic participation in that space. This approach makes inhabited space something to reflect upon and to "open mental maps to analysis" of those spaces (133).

Brooke and McIntosh claim that "initially, writers need to become accustomed to seeing themselves *in a place*, that is, they need to become aware of the various ways location (literal and mental) creates their understanding of landscape, culture, class, race, and gender, and surrounds them with local issues and local possibilities" (132). What better place to exercise one's cognitive and rhetorical faculties than in a community literacy project? By definition, community literacy seeks to engage people in writing, communication, and civic life. Therefore, place-based composition seems inseparable from community literacy initiatives. But is it comprehensive enough?

Another pedagogical framework with which to approach community literacy may be ecocomposition, as envisioned by Sidney Dobrin and Christian Weisser in *Ecocomposition, Theoretical and Pedagogical Approaches*. These authors view ecocomposition as an "investigation of the total relations of discourse both to its organic and inorganic environment and to the study of all of the complex interrelationships between the human activity of writing and all of the conditions of the struggle for existence" (13). Much like place-based composition and education, ecocomposition is underpinned by the interconnected nature of things. Dobrin claims it is "the study of relationships: between individual writers and their surrounding environments, between writers and texts, between texts and culture, between ideology and discourse, and between language and the world" (12). Truly an ecological perspective on a writer's/citizen's place in the world, ecocomposition places the community literacy practitioner at the heart of an evolving matrix rich in economic, social, and political dynamisms that require deeper understanding if real and lasting progress is to be made.

While this is a completely appropriate and laudable approach to any composition classroom or community literacy program with far-reaching benefits for students, participating community members, teachers, and the larger world, one must ask if it is comprehensive enough. Dobrin himself poses similar questions in "Writing Takes Place," in an attempt to define ecocomposition. Clearly recognizing its lack of full methodological development, he asks pointedly if our primacy of language has not separated us from the natural world. In doing so, he sees ecocomposition as "the place in which ecology and rhetoric and composition can converge to better explore the relationships between language, writing, and discourse; and between nature, place, environment, and locations" (12). Regardless of the more fully developed, ecological scope in composition that scholars like Dobrin and Weisser call for, one gets the sense that a more critical pedagogical approach may be necessary, especially when working in a community literacy setting. In light of this, ecopedagogy may be a more comprehensive strategy when working within the field of community literacy.

Richard Kahn, in *Critical Pedagogy, Ecoliteracy, and Planetary Crisis*, discusses the roots of ecopedagogy as representing a "profound transformation in the radical educational and political project derived from the work of Paulo Freire known as *critical pedagogy*" (18). He claims that ecopedagogy seeks two aims: (1) to humanize experience based on an ecologically oriented politics that stands in opposition to global neoliberalism and imperialism, and (2) to develop a cohesive ecoliteracy and realization of "culturally relevant forms of knowledge grounded in normative concepts such as sustainability, planetarity, and biophilia" (18). With these formidable goals in mind, ecopedagogy takes ecocomposition and critical pedagogy and infuses them with a militant passion geared toward social change.

The Strength of Ecopedagogy

It is fair to say that a large proportion of community literacy practitioners are geared toward civic engagement and social change. Given the ecological nature of writing and the broader range of literacy skills, ecopedagogy is a unique and powerful pedagogical strategy in which to frame an approach to service learning programs and other activities engaged in the goals of community literacy.

An important component of ecopedagogy is its view of environmental crisis as an essential pedagogical concern. Scholars such as Richard Kahn consider ecopedagogy as a way to profoundly transform education and in turn, make for a more sustainable world. Ecopedagogy supports sustainability by helping to construct curricular frameworks that contribute to ecological, political, and social policies. In the field of community literacy, this works well to inform scholarly approach and program development because it upholds similar values that see the exploration of social injustice, educational inequities, and marginalized populations as a central areas of focus.

Just as community literacy practitioners such as Linda Flower focus on facilitating community conversations within marginalized groups of people to work toward building solutions and democratizing knowledge, ecopedagogy is a critical pedagogy that seeks to do much the same with the additional focus on environmental literacy as the underpinning of a healthy human society. Ecopedagogy also seeks to shed light on systemic injustices that squelch individual voices that make up community and inhibit solution finding.

The philosophy of Richard Kahn shares common values with community literacy practitioners; he points a critical finger at the silencing of communities and the current trend toward social and environmental disaster by a "global technocapitalist infrastructure that relies upon market-based and functionalist versions of technoliteracy to instantiate and augment its socioeconomic and cultural control" (9). Such a critical pedagogy can be immensely powerful in examining communities and the social, institutional, and political structures that impact them. These structures may inhibit fair and just solutions from being implemented and the democratic knowledge that arises from community conversation can help identify this.

A Strategy for Rural Literacy Programs

I would like now to consider the applicability of ecopedagogy to rural literacy programs, particularly because rural environments may have unique literacy needs and challenges. In "Rural Literacies," Kim Donehower, Charlotte Hogg, and Eileen Schell view literacy as inseparable from notions of sustainability. While they do not utilize the term ecopedagogy in their analysis of rural literacies, they explicitly state that their approach is underpinned by a conception that involves a "multidimensional definition of sustainability, one that is informed by ecological, economic, political, and social factors and the interdependence of these factors" (6). Clearly an ecopedagogical approach, their goal to "promote models of citizen participation that will ensure the future of rural communities and spark potential solidarity between rural, urban, and suburban communities" is admirable and rich with potential for community writing projects aimed at broadening and deepening understanding about what it means to be a rural community member as well as a global citizen (8).

An important aspect of engaging public pedagogy and citizen participation is to connect teaching and learning to social empowerment. Donehower, Hogg, and Schell urge that a critical step in achieving this in rural communities is to interrogate "constructions and representations of rural people and life" and analyze how they match up with characterizations and stereotypes of rural life and literacy (9). A global understanding of where communities fit in is also crucial because it provides a deeper contextual foothold. In order for students and citizens to move toward literacies, they need to be part of a global conversation. In order for people to understand how and when to "resist, critique, and imagine alternatives to the official logic of neoliberalism, the global movement toward increased privatization of public services and toward a market economy dominated by predatory multinational corporations" citizens must have literacy skills (10). Ecopedagogy can help achieve this deeper contextual foothold to inform their decisions.

How do rural citizens take up the challenges to "resist, critique, and imagine alternatives" in their communities? How do literacy skills in rural communities rise to these challenges? Literacy skills as taught in standard public education have been subject to endless scrutiny, and regardless of how they "measure up," scholars are considering this potential lack of skill with a fresh perspective—one that seeks to empower rural citizens. But in doing so, students, teachers, parents, and community members are often faced with a reality that is deeply ingrained in our psyche: that moving *away* from one's community is a measure of success. Contemporary economics has witnessed for decades the inclination to identify success with migration; migration to larger, more cosmopolitan cities has come to be viewed as synonymous with success. This trend may have not only created a false sense of security for prospective job seekers; it also may send the message that to stay where one is located equals lack of success.

When rural communities not only witness but anticipate the exodus of their youthful population, this can have lasting and damaging effects. The work and community building that is going on is devalued and a sense of historical association is lost as a community's young citizens seek meaningful lives elsewhere. The lack of connection and understanding of place and one's history in public education has indeed created several harmful practices, including reduced empathy for real places and people, disregard for cultural heritage and its preservation, and the creation of one's own identity in relation to accountability and sustainability as citizens. In his essay, "Voices of Young Citizens: Rural Citizenship, Schools, and Public Policy," Robert Brooke claims that "rural communities need a new kind of citizen, and rural education ought to help shape such citizens" (161). Brooke claims that mainstream education, as predominantly practiced, "points elsewhere: to history happening in other parts of the world, to migration as the means of personal advancement in the corporate industrial complex, to an ineffective form of citizenship" (163).

How can education, literacy programs, and their unique pedagogies, aid in Brooke's assertion that rural education ought to help shape new kinds of citizens? In shaping such citizens, the odds that rural communities will improve and thrive are greatly increased. Brooke goes on to say that "if rural communities are to survive into the next century as places where vibrant, thriving populaces can live well and grow, then rural citizenship needs to become more active, rhetorically effective, and politically savvy" (161). To do so, education must clearly focus its curriculum on more than preparing youth to seek meaningful lives elsewhere without questioning and rhetorically analyzing the world around them.

Utilizing rural education to support the development of this "new kind of citizen," Brooke details what he refers to as a place-based project in rural Nebraska. Although not explicitly labeled as such, the project also serves as an example of ecopedagogy applied to a rural community literacy effort. Entitled "Voices of Young Citizens," this project was the result of a collaboration between community partners that had previously worked together: the Nebraska Writing Project, the Nebraska Humanities Council, and NET-TV. Based on a previously filmed series depicting regional leaders exploring questions about the survival of rural communities in Nebraska, producer William Kelly made the decision to follow up with discussions with rural youth (Brooke 167). The project then focused on finding teachers within schools that had already implemented place-based education in their curricula to help develop a plan for the program. The aim of the project was to give students the opportunity to create their own public rhetorical space to discuss issues they found pertinent to the growth and survival of their communities.

Giving rural youth a chance to develop their own rhetorical space for public television, Brooke asks, "What kind of persuasive, public action do young people create?" (168). Focusing on senior students from Nebraskan schools, Brooke notes that students were making connections for themselves between rural communities and economics, their own families, and the larger global economics impacting rural economies and communities, as well as migration and economic opportunity (169). From five different high schools, the following issues arose: dwindling economic opportunities, the nature of community, reliance on overused local natural resources, rural depopulation and disappearing elements of rural life, and water usage and economic controversies across the Great Plains (167).

In exploring these issues with family members, teachers, friends, and other community members, Brooke emphasizes that the issues selected by the students were "also identified as crucial by the state's business community" and that the issues also fit "into the national pattern of rural net migration loss" (169). As a community literacy effort, this project involved many community participants with a diverse level of literacy skills from professional TV producers to students. In identifying issues affecting their rural communities, students analyzed the issues through an ecological lens. The very nature of giving students the opportunity to create their own rhetorical space required community involvement and analysis of their place within a larger social matrix.

As Brooke notes, it is not solely the education of a community's youthful student population with their newly acquired literacy skills that point them elsewhere; the lack of meaningful connection and commitment to the places we inhabit often force people away. Community literacy efforts that span the population and pull people together through shared commitment and civic participation in their communities are essential to combat these tendencies of disconnection and distance. The "Voices of Young Citizens" project serves as an example of solidifying community partnerships and raising the stakes for students involved, which creates in them a sense of shared meaning and purpose.

Contributing to these notions and their negative consequences are the under-representation and often false representation of actual rural communities. In their introduction to *Reclaiming the Rural, Essays on Literacy, Rhetoric, and Pedagogy*, Kim Donehower, Charlotte Hogg, and Eileen Schell claim that what results from neoliberalism, which gives "markets primacy over people," is "under-represented constituencies, such as rural residents who lack lobbying power, have difficulty asserting their needs and values" (8). Increasingly, rural people and the geographical locations they inhabit are viewed as "economic, political, or military resources" (9). It is in this rhetorical space that ecopedagogy may contribute to a more thorough understanding of the challenges faced by rural literacy programs.

Donehower, Hogg, and Schell claim that "to avoid treating rural areas as sites for resource exploitation, sites of cheap labor, or as dumping grounds for toxic substances or institutions that no one else wants in their backyards (prisons, for instance) means identifying with rural life and people" (9). But how might literacy practitioners successfully identify with rural life and people? In reviewing ecopedagogy's aims as presented by Richard Kahn, it becomes apparent that its aims would not only support, but strengthen goals common to community literacy practitioners, to which identifying with the lives of the people in the community is paramount. According to Kahn's assertions, in seeking to "humanize experience based on an ecologically oriented politics that stands in opposition to global neoliberalism and imperialism," it becomes evident that ecopedagogy digs deeper into the underlying reasons and assumptions for difficulties in rural communities.

For example, rural communities often see increased levels of poverty, lack of education and opportunity, and a feeling of helplessness and lack of identity, as well as a desire to migrate to centers of civilization. These trends can all be explored further when viewed under an ecopedagogical lens. Developing a cohesive ecoliteracy and realization of, as Richard Kahn points out, "culturally relevant forms of knowledge grounded in normative concepts such as sustainability, planetarity, and biophilia" (18) can only result in more meaningful constructs arising in rural communities, as well as a deeper understanding of the challenges they face. Ecoliteracy is seen as an essential goal embedded within ecopedagogy. In "From Education for Sustainable Development to Ecopedagogy: Sustaining Capitalism or Sustaining Life?" Richard Kahn sees ecopedagogy as a "total liberation pedagogy for sustaining life" because of its potential for recreation and reconstruction of the very notions of what constitutes human society (11).

Bringing ecopedagogy and its critical ecoliteracy to bear on issues that plague rural communities holds tremendous potential to benefit not only everyday citizens but communities as a whole, including the ecological matrix that supports the very basics of life. Kahn, in discussing the goals of the "Earth Charter Initiative," a document arising from the first Earth Summit in Rio de Janeiro in 1992, emphasizes the importance of thrusting "environmental and socioeconomic/political problems together in one light and demanding long-term, integrated responses to the growing planetary social and ecological problems" (7). He says that three types of ecoliteracy need development if we are to build just and sustainable communities: the technical or functional, the cultural, and the critical (9). Functional ecoliteracy deals with basic environmental literacy as it is relevant to communal human impact including geology, ecology, etc., which most public education has until very recently been seriously lacking. For rural community literacy practitioners, integrating bioregional literacy with rhetorical analysis is not only imperative, but it can make for a more interesting engagement for both practitioners and participants.

Rural literacy practitioners, while clearly holding firmly to established literacy goals, might infuse their composition pedagogy with this more rhetorically focused agenda that invests participants in finding solid solutions to local concerns. In "From Education for Sustainable Development to Ecopedagogy: Sustaining Capitalism or Sustaining Life?" Kahn once again pushes the merging of critical pedagogy and ecoliteracy and argues that ecopedagogy holds the potential to move environmental education beyond

> its discursive marginality and a real hope for an ecological and planetary society could be sustained through the widespread development of radical socioeconomic critiques and the sort of emancipatory life practices that could move beyond those programmatically offered by the culture industries and the State. (8)

In so doing, rural literacy becomes a place of rhetorical empowerment—a place of claimed identity, sustainability, and real hope.

Practitioners need to aid students in understanding the rhetorical spaces that exist and in defining their own. People need the literacy skills to do this and to develop themselves as community members and citizens as part of a larger persuasive public. Just as many minority groups are marginalized, many rural students denied visibility because the cultural environment from which they emerge is insignificant in comparison to larger metropolises. Robert Brooke acknowledges that his own community in rural Nebraska could "benefit from more citizens who can, *make* persuasive public rhetorical space" (163). Literacy practitioners would, I think, be hard-pressed to find a community that could not benefit from such a citizenry.

Clearly, an ecopedagogical approach to rural literacy programs is a comprehensive strategy that could be utilized when working within the field of community literacy and could benefit from the addition of a rhetorical model that helps to frame the inquiries that a community literacy program might encounter. The rhetorical model of Lorraine Higgins, Elenore Long, and Linda Flower as proposed in "Community Literacy: A Rhetorical Model for Personal and Public Inquiry" is one such model that may work productively in rural settings. Their model consists of "assessing the rhetorical situation, creating a local public, developing participants' rhetorical capacities, and supporting personal and public transformation through the circulation of alternative texts and practices" (170) and is a clear framework in which to place ecopedagogical inquiries. Consisting of elements that are essential in any community literacy effort, the model could provide structure and cohesion but is not without its own challenges as explored in the following section.

Challenges as Explored by Higgins, Flower, and Long

In working with rural literacy communities to potentially help others gain "rhetorical capacities" regarding issues that affect the community as a whole, practitioners might view "eliciting situated knowledge, engaging difference in dialogue, and constructing and reflecting upon wise options" as a critical foundation upon which to base pedagogy and practice. This may prove effective in any literacy project but especially one that is tied up in contentious misunderstanding (178). As previously discussed, rural communities are often not only sites of misunderstanding, but of misrepresentation and under-representation, resulting in the community's actual needs and values being overlooked. By assessing the rhetorical situation in hopes of what Higgins, Long, and Flower refer to as "developing participants' rhetorical capacities," (170) ecopedagogical inquiry could be a grounding experience—one that attempts to instill an ecological worldview that benefits one's own community as well as the larger community. It is also a pedagogy that recognizes the inherent challenges of such an undertaking and can only serve the practitioners and participants in furthering constructive dialogue.

Lorraine Higgins, Elenore Long, and Linda Flower refer to developing rhetorical capacities and participants' "situated knowledge " as a "resource for transformed understanding and wise action" (179). Ethical issues of primary concern in this type of literacy community center around two things: (1) citizens' motivation to help create a "local public" as defined by Higgins, Long, and Flower, and (2) engaging a truly deliberative democracy (176). The ethical challenges surrounding creating a local public with which to engage becomes problematic, as it can only exist if citizens in a particular area are "willing to lend their attention, to participate in the discourse."

They go on to say that "in a democracy, one of the most necessary but problem-ridden functions of a public is to deliberate about shared social concerns" (175).

Given trends of migration and lack of connection to place, one would have to wonder how participative a rural public might be. Practitioners may be surprised by participants' desire to rhetorically analyze the situations they find themselves within communities that typically lack economic, political, and social support. Higgins, Long, and Flower contend that assessing the rhetorical situation in local publics ought to involve the following considerations: "configuring the *problem space* or object of deliberation, identifying relevant *stakeholders* in the community, assessing existing *venues* for public problem solving, and analyzing *literate practices* used to represent and address problems and the way these practices structure stakeholder *participation*" (171). They view public deliberation as a "cognitive-social-cultural *activity*" which echoes the conception of ecoliteracy as an experienced action-based literacy. Engaging citizens in a rural local public in such deliberative discourse could only deepen understanding and community connection.

Regardless of the pedagogical strategy community literacy practitioners use to build their courses or programs, they must first investigate what Higgins, Long, and Flower identify as a challenge in creating a deliberative democracy – identifying shared concerns of a local public. The shared concerns in rural communities may be forthcoming only after constructive dialogue begins and increased rhetorical capacity is evident. The rich and varied work in rural communities available for community literacy practitioners seems unending. However, several questions arise in investigating a rural literacy community: What types of things constitute shared concerns? How do levels of literacy compare with other populations? And how successful are deliberative democracies in more isolated communities?

Donehower, Hogg, and Schell advocate a "critical, public pedagogy that questions and renegotiates the relationships among rural, urban, and suburban people" (155). Recall that ecopedagogy also calls for the critical questioning of rhetorical situations and making connections between culturally relevant forms of knowledge. Its emphasis on humanizing experience based on ecologically-oriented politics mutually reinforces the goals of the model proposed by Higgins, Long, and Flower while digging deeper into the multi-faceted layers of human societies and the connections that can propel communities forward or hinder the very stability they depend on. Even with the challenges literacy practitioners might face in rural communities as outlined above, ecopedagogy still serves as a foundational springboard from which to frame questions of literacy, empowerment, justice, and community building because it views everything in terms of relationship and interconnectivity.

Conclusion

In exploring and unraveling the goals of ecopedagogy, it is clear that it provides a dynamic and viable option for community literacy practitioners, and in particular, those whose work focuses primarily on rural communities. Merging critical pedagogy with radical ecoliteracy, ecopedagogy holds the potential to not only encourage multiculturally relevant forms of knowledge but also to analyze, critique, and deconstruct the cultural texts that surround us. According to Richard Kahn, the kind of ambitious ecoliteracy that is embedded within ecopedagogy involves

> empirical and lived action-based literacies but it also requires ideologically critiquing and deconstructing various forms of cultural texts – including print materials like books, magazines, and newspaper articles; video texts such as films, television shows and other videographic forms; pictographical representations ranging from museum art pieces to t-shirt images; and digital texts of the Internet and association information-communication technologies. (14)

In light of this broader conception and its embrace of action-based literacies and lived experience, utilizing ecopedagogy in a community literacy setting offers a rich and diverse palette for participants and practitioners alike. It also elevates the local public to a space of deep and valued consideration; as stated by Higgins, Long, and Flower, "local publics not only spark personal transformation but public change" (193).

The primary goal of community literacy practitioners in rural programs is to develop collaborative and deliberative democracies, thereby helping citizens view themselves as part of a larger community and begin to understand the importance of living based on the interconnectivity of all life. An integral component of these goals is to help people see that individuals in a community are capable of powerful rhetorical action. Rural community members may view themselves as independent and isolated, when in reality, they are capable of taking powerful rhetorical stances. By debunking myths surrounding rural literacies that prevail in the scholarship and working against urban biases, community literacy programs founded upon ecopedagogical strategies can inform and empower both scholars and community members.

Works Cited

Brooke, Robert. "Voices of Young Citizens: Rural Citizenship, Schools, and Public Policy." *Reclaiming the Rural: Essays on Literacy, Rhetoric, and Pedagogy*. Carbondale: Southern Illinois University Press, 2012. 161-173. Print.

Cushman, Ellen. "Service Learning as the New English Studies." *Beyond English, Inc.: Curricular Reform in a Global Economy*. Chicago: Heinemann, 2002. 204-218. Print.

Dobrin, Sidney. *Postcomposition*. Carbondale: Southern Illinois University Press, 2011. Print.

Dobrin, Sidney I., and Christopher J. Keller. *Writing Environments*. Albany: State University of New York Press, 2005. Print.

Donehower, Kim, Charlotte Hogg, and Eileen E. Schell. *Rural Literacies*. Carbondale: Southern Illinois University Press, 2007. Print.

———. *Reclaiming the Rural: Essays on Literacy, Rhetoric, and Pedagogy*. Carbondale: Southern Illinois University Press, 2012. Print.

Faigley, Lester. "The Changing Political Landscape of Composition Studies." *Fragments of Rationality: Postmodernity and the Subject of Composition*. Pittsburgh: University of Pittsburgh Press, 1992. 48-79. Print.

George, Diana. "The Word on the Street: Public Discourse in a Culture of Disconnect." *Writing and Community Engagement: A Critical Sourcebook*. Boston: Bedford/St. Martin's, 2010. 50-60. Print.

Kahn, Richard V.. *Critical Pedagogy, Ecoliteracy, & Planetary Crisis: The Ecopedagogy Movement*. New York: Peter Lang, 2010. Print.

Keller, Christopher J., and Christian R. Weisser. *The Locations of Composition*. Albany: State University of New York Press, 2007. Print.

Orr, David W.. *Earth in Mind: On Education, Environment, and the Human Prospect*. Washington, DC: Island Press, 1994. Print.

Owens, Derek. *Composition and Sustainability: Teaching for a Threatened Generation*. Urbana, Ill.: National Council of Teachers of English, 2001. Print.

Powell, Douglas, and John Paul Tassoni. *Composing Other Spaces*. Cresskill, NJ: Hampton Press, 2009. Print.

Sobel, David. *Childhood and Nature Design Principles for Educators*. Portland, Maine, Stenhouse Publishers, 2008. Print.

_____. *Place-Based Education: Connecting Classrooms & Communities*. Great Barrington, MA: The Orion Society, 2004. Print.

Weisser, Christian R., and Sidney I. Dobrin. *Ecocomposition: Theoretical and Pedagogical Approaches*. Albany, New York: State University Of New York Press, 2001. Print.

Rhonda Davis is an adjunct instructor of Composition and Rhetoric in the English Department at Northern Kentucky University with special interests in the ecology of writing and its intersection with community literacy.

community literacy journal

Book and New Media Reviews

From the Book & New Media Review Editor's Desk

Jim Bowman

In our capacities as civically engaged community members, critical language scholars, and reflective professional educators, daily work in a pluralistic society regularly and inevitably implicates us in discourses of complex cultural difference. Whether our context involves literacy work with refugee communities or the teaching of writing in higher education, similar challenges over access, power, and language can vex our professional practices. Recent scholarship in literacy studies reviewed in this issue covers an ambitious host of questions. For example, what does it mean to teach language and literacy for all members of our society? How do we do this, and, for that matter, how do we measure the meaning of our efforts? What sort of rhetorical flexibility is requisite for a scholar-educator who wishes to realize a vision of social justice in historically inequitable institutions? Difficult questions deserve sustained, reflective, scholarly treatment. Fortunately, a wealth of resources avails itself to those determined to better understand and respond to the social and cultural differences that produce distinct literacies in a society like our own.

This issue's keyword essay sets the tone for a collection of review essays that extend our capacity to respond critically to the many challenges of teaching language and literacy in a world of cultural difference and asymmetrical relations of power. Michael MacDonald's keyword essay on *refugee literacy* describes experiences that he concludes "do not easily mesh with dominant models of literacy, citizenship, and community, but [...] nonetheless provide a compelling and important inroad to better understanding literacy in global and local contexts." Abigail Montgomery's look at John Duffy's *Writing from These Roots: Literacy in a Hmong-American Community* represents a powerful illustration of the ways one historically distinct cultural group has responded to local literacies through acts of critical appropriation. The final three reviews turn their attention to some of the challenges of realizing social justice in institutions of higher education. Leah Durán's take on *Affirming Students' Right to Their Own Language* demonstrates how critical practitioners of today's college writing classrooms can deploy a host of nuanced strategies designed to realize the promise of NCTE's 1973 egalitarian vision. For those of us looking to strengthen community connections between high schools and universities, Lance Langdon's critique of two texts, Maisha Fisher's *Writing in Rhythm: Spoken Word Poets in Urban Classrooms* and Korina Jocson's *Youth Poets: Empowering Literacies In and Out of Schools*, reminds us of the power of poetry as a source of inspiration and motivation. The final review, Lance Hendrickson's engaging summation of the *The Inaugural Summit of the National Consortium of Writing Across Communities*, held in New Mexico in July 2012, testifies to "the hard work of imagining" and its potential rewards for communities across our country.

Keywords: Refugee Literacy
Michael MacDonald

The subject of refugee experience poses compelling problematics for the study of community literacy. Yet, community literacy projects that support language acquisition, cultural orientation, and cross-cultural communication are some of the most important resources available to newly resettled refugees. Refugee students and adult learners arrive in the U.S. and are forced to learn English as quickly as possible while also having to figure out the new and complicated bureaucratic trappings of finding a job, making doctors' appointments, and enrolling in school. Refugees, however, cannot be considered one homogeneous group, and the issues surrounding refugee resettlement and community literacy play out in a myriad of ways. Community literacy research, particularly of the ethnographic variety, teaches us that very little can be generalized or concluded about literacy practice or literacy acquisition from one community to another. This observation cannot be overstated when it comes to the literacy issues faced by refugee communities in the U.S. In this keywords essay, I outline several aspects of refugee experience that carry important implications for understanding literacy in the contexts of refugee resettlement. While this essay is not meant to describe *how* refugees gain literacy or what their literacy practices look like—such work requires ethnographic study—instead, I offer a range of ways for talking about literacy in relation to refugee experience, particularly through the lenses of the interdisciplinary field of refugee studies and rhetoric and composition. Despite the implications refugee experience might have for understanding literacy in global contexts, the perspectives of refugees have been given only cursory attention. A synthesis of contemporary scholarship, however, affords us sufficient grounds to enact a more reflective, ethical, and responsible approach to understanding literacy-learning in refugee communities.

Refugee studies is a distinctly interdisciplinary field that emerged as a "whole new" object of study after World War II (Malkki 497), and many scholars have described the twentieth century as the "age of the refugee" (Lewellen 171). Given the amount of forced displacement so far in the twenty-first century, we are not any closer to amending that reality. Refugee studies includes a wide range of approaches to the study of refugee experience, including the theorization of refugee identity in contradistinction to citizenship (Nyers), the particular experiences of refugee children (Watters), the implications gender has on displacement and resettlement (Grewal), the study of the interview process crucial to the granting of asylum (Bohmer and Schuman), and the study of how refugees are perceived by the international community and general public (Malkki). As Charles Watters explains, merely the topic of migration is a "wide-ranging, multifaceted and highly complex phenomenon" that is only made more complicated when the transnational movement of people is forced (9).

Refugee identity is vexed by several competing logics. In practical terms, the word "refugee" denotes a legal status that marks one eligible to receive humanitarian aid, particularly in the form of asylum, though much of the research on refugees agrees that refugee status is difficult to apply evenly across different experiences and contexts. The practice is fraught with inconsistency. The United Nations provides a conventional definition: an individual who seeks asylum in another nation-state due to a "well-founded fear of being persecuted" (UNHCR 16). Implementations of this definition, however, vary from one governing body to another and, according to refugee studies scholar Peter Nyers, operate according to processes "deeply rooted in political and ideological calculations," making legal refugee status a form of aid that is unevenly distributed (13).

On the policy level, Nyers observes that the category of *refugee* operates according to a "state logic," or what "can be understood as a power of capture" wherein "subjects of the classification regime of 'refugeeness' are caged within a depoliticized humanitarian space" (xiii). The state logic, in other words, regards refugees as one homogeneous mass of people, and the "depoliticized space" in which they are "caged" constrains both their physical and rhetorical mobility. According to state logic, refugees are measured against that which they are not: "adult," "historical actor," "sovereign citizen" (xiv). Individual refugee identity is only acknowledged during the process of determining who is eligible to receive asylum, a process heavily burdened by ideology. For instance, Inderpal Grewal examines how governing bodies might use gender to restructure policy, to determine within a given displaced population who is "more" deserving of aid, resettlement, or protection (159).

Malkki argues, however, that refugees can often come to "appropriate the category as a vital, positive dimension of their collective identity in exile" (377). One way in which refugees express this more positive view is through telling stories of their experience. Since both Malkki and Nyers refer to the "depoliticizing" tendency of governing bodies, we might tentatively term this positive understanding of refugeeness a kind of "political logic," which draws attention to the historical, political, and communal aspects of refugee experience and its implications for different forms of agency. Even the consideration of refugee identity as positive can rebuke state logic because it immediately contradicts constructions of the refugee figure as a passive object of aid. The stories refugees tell of their own experience are both personal and political, historicizing and concrete, and represent one important intersection between literacy research and refugee studies.

As noted earlier, these logics compete with one another, and the state logic can often silence or appropriate the stories refugees tell. However, the "state," as Nyers uses the term, does not only imply nation-state authority or jurisdiction but includes governing bodies such as the United Nations, non-governmental organizations (NGOs), charitable organizations, and networks of volunteer aid workers, religious organizations, the Red Cross, and so forth—a panoply of actors who govern and bureaucratize refugee subjects as they cross various manifestations of borders. This is analogous to Foucault's description of "governmentality." According to Foucault, governmentality refers to the "ensemble formed by institutions, procedures, analyses, reflections, and tactics that allow the exercise" of power (108). In this light, the state logic can be taken to reflect the "ensemble" of attitudes and political processes which produce knowledge about refugees—especially in the way the discourses of power that "cage" refugee subjects are not solely used by the state in its official capacity but also to shape popular attitudes toward refugee identity: political, economic, and military agendas are realized through refugee discourse. Of course, the prevailing attitude is that refugees are victims, are objects of pity, and because they are sometimes entirely dependent upon aid (when in a refugee camp, for example), they are often seen as a burden on the system. The popular attitude is that only the developed nations of the First World may aid or uplift them. In this way, the concept of "governmentality" points toward the many competing logics, including neoliberal capitalism, that shape public perception of refugee communities.

Literacy research has several important implications for popular perceptions of refugees. One implication concerns the alleged link between literacy and economic development. Harvey J. Graff argues that this, the most persistent of myths about literacy, seems to have been "unreflectively incorporated into the principal narratives of the rise of the West and the triumph of democracy, modernization, and progress. Indeed, literacy was equated with those qualities, each seemingly the cause of the other in a confused causal order" (113-14). The assumed connection between progress and literacy places an explicit emphasis on English literacy in particular. Reading and writing are generally regarded as empowering, but nothing is seen as more empowering or uplifting as English, the steward of democracy and neoliberal capitalism. Graff's work is crucial for understanding the intersections between literacy and refugee experience because the countries from which refugees are resettled are often misperceived as backward, deficient, illiterate, preliterate, resistant to assimilation, or underdeveloped. Ethnographic studies of literacy in global contexts such as those done by David Barton and Brian Street address such representations. Street's work on the "ideological model" of literacy, in particular, is helpful for deconstructing the dominant assumption that literacy is inherently empowering or benign and that certain forms of literacy are universally valuable.

Out of such research has come a critique of the perceived link between literacy and citizenship. This relationship is tenuous because, as Amy J. Wan argues, uses of the term "citizenship" are often "ambient" in nature but should be viewed as context-bound rather than universal (29). Wendy Hesford's work also poses problems for studies of citizenship because she argues that despite embracing a more global perspective, scholars have continued to "take for granted the nation-state and citizen-subject as units of analysis" (788). This is a helpful reminder that students and adult learners who identify as refugees occupy a liminal space in the minds of both researchers and the general public.

Deborah Brandt's conceptualization of "literacy sponsorship" is one of the most useful approaches for understanding literacy and refugee experience. Brandt defines "sponsors of literacy" as "any agents, local or distant, concrete or abstract, who enable, support, teach, model, as well as recruit, regulate, suppress, or withhold literacy – and gain advantage by it in some way" (166). In the lives of refugees, literacy sponsors come in the form of aid workers, case managers, volunteers, tutors, and teachers, as well as aid and charity organizations who promote literacy as a means for attaining citizenship, education, and employment. Literacy not only takes the form of English language acquisition, but also includes cultural literacy through orientation classes and volunteer mentoring programs. This is the main form of contact new refugees have with other communities. Literacy sponsorship is a framework for studying the many asymmetrical relations of power pertaining to community literacy projects in refugee communities.

Studies in rhetoric offer a useful approach for examining the state and political logics discussed by Nyers and Malkki, particularly in relation to the stories that refugees tell and how they choose to tell them. In "Rhetorics of Displacement: Constructing Identities in Forced Relocations," Katrina M. Powell observes how "displacement narratives written *about* the displaced often go through a process of *othering* whereby they blame the victim, have particular notions of citizenry, and at worse, dehumanize the displaced through metaphors of savagery"; in turn, stories of refugee experience can provide evidence of how individual refugees can strategically "speak back to" these discourses of power (original emphasis 302). Rhetorical analysis of stories written by and about refugees is another productive intersection between refugee studies and literacy research. Carol Bohmer and Amy Shuman take up similar work in *Rejecting Refugees*, a case study analysis that examines the policies and procedures used to evaluate applications for refugee status, most notably the process of resettlement interviews. These are processes in which the rhetorics of power that "cage" refugees play out most visibly.

While this essay is not an exhaustive review of the intersections between literacy and refugee studies, I have tried to present a tentative outline of the issues most relevant to community literacy. There are many studies across a range of disciplines that address specific refugee populations and their experiences with literacy and education. And, looking through the growing list of "keywords" essays in the *Community Literacy Journal*, several keywords appear immediately applicable to literacy projects in refugee communities. For example, many refugees come to the U.S. as adults or are too old for high school when they are resettled and must pursue a G.E.D., and as William Carney suggests, *adult literacy* is an important concept for understanding the lives of English-language learners and new immigrants. Stephanie Vie's description of *qualitative research* speaks to the heterogeneity of refugee experience that requires on-the-ground observation rather than sweeping generalization. When we conduct research in refugee communities, though, we also participate in them, and this has implications for our understanding of *reciprocity*. Miller, Wheeler, and White demonstrate that the relationships researchers form with the communities they work in are important for approaches to social justice. Common amongst these keyword essays is an insistence on attending to the many contexts under which community literacy research takes place in an effort to foster ethical and responsible relationships with the communities in which we choose to do our work. As a keyword, *refugee literacy* describes experiences that do not easily mesh with dominant models of literacy, citizenship, and community, but it does nonetheless provide a compelling and important inroad to better understanding literacy in global and local contexts.

Works Cited

Bohmer, Carol, and Amy Schuman. *Rejecting Refugees: Political Asylum in the 21st Century*. London: Routledge, 2008. Print.

Barton, David. "The Social Nature of Writing." *Writing in the Community*. Eds. David Barton and Roz Ivanic. Newbury Park: Sage Publications, Inc., 1991. 1-13. Print.

Brandt, Deborah. "Sponsors of Literacy." *College Composition and Communication* 49.2 (1998):165-185. Print.

Carney, William. "Keywords: Adult Literacy." *Community Literacy Journal* 4.2 (2010): 100-04. Print.

Graff, Harvey J. *Literacy Myths, Legacies, and Lessons*. New Brunswick: Transaction Publishers, 2011. Print.

Grewal, Inderpal. *Transnational America: Feminisms, Diasporas, Neoliberalisms*. Durham: Duke UP: 2005. Print.

Hesford, Wendy. "Global Turns and Cautions in Rhetoric and Composition Studies." *PMLA* 126.3 (2006): 787-801. Print.

Lewellen, Ted. C. *The Anthropology of Globalization: Cultural Anthropology Enters the 21st Century*. Westport: Bergin & Garvey, 2002. Print.

Malkki, Liisa. "Refugees and Exile: From 'Refugee Studies' to the National Order of Things." *Annual Review of Anthropology* 24 (1995). 494-523. Print.

---. "Speechless Emissaries: Refugees, Humanitarianism, and Dehistoricization" *Cultural Anthropology* 11.3 (1996). 377-404. Print.

Miller, Elisabeth, Anne Wheeler, and Stephanie White. "Keywords: Reciprocity." *Community Literacy Journal* 5.2 (2011): 171-177. Print.

Powell, Katrina M. "Rhetorics of Displacement: Constructing Identities in Forced Relocations." *College English* 74.4 (2012): 299-324. Print.

Street, Brian. "Orality and Literacy as Ideological Constructions: Some Problems in Cross-cultural Studies." *Culture and History* 2 (1987): 7-30. Print.

UNHCR. "Text of the 1967 Protocol Relating to the Status of Refugees." *Convention and Protocol Relating to the Status of Refugees*. The United Nations High Commission for Refugees. 2007. 16-52. Print.

Vie, Stephanie. "Keywords: Qualitative Research." *Community Literacy Journal* 5.1 (2010): 175-180. Print.

Wan, Amy J. "In the Name of Citizenship: The Writing Classroom and the Promise of Citizenship." *College English* 74.1 (2011): 28-49. Print.

Watters, Charles. *Refugee Children: Towards the Next Horizon*. London: Routledge, 2008. Print.

Writing from These Roots: Literacy in a Hmong-American Community
John M. Duffy
Honolulu: U of Hawaii P, 2007. 241 pp.
ISBN: 978-0-8248-3615-3. $21.

Reviewed by Abigail L. Montgomery
Blue Ridge Community College, Weyers Cave, VA

The immigration debates of recent years have touched all of our communities and classrooms. In my hometown, government, family, church, and other relocation efforts have created extraordinary diversity for a rural town of 40,000, with the largest immigrant groups coming from the Middle East, formerly Soviet republics, and Mexico. Our high school represents over 40 languages spoken. My college's students reflect this diversity. I attend a church that conducts English, Spanish, and Arabic services and offers English lessons. John M. Duffy's *Writing from These Roots: Literacy in a Hmong-American Community* is an engaging and informative look, through the lens of literacy and rhetorical education, at two communities'—one town and one ethnic group—responses to similar circumstances in the mid-to-late twentieth century.

Duffy explores literacy education and public rhetoric in Wasau, Wisconsin's Hmong-American community, placing many individuals' stories—gathered through extensive personal interviews as well as archival research—within a broader survey of their literate, political, and geographic histories. He aims to "[connect] ethnographic, historical, and theoretical perspectives" (10) and succeeds in admirable fashion. Duffy also grounds the book in an explicitly rhetorical understanding of literacy, literate practices, and literate acts. He describes "the rhetorical character of literacy, or the ways in which a writing system can offer a conception of identity and position" (42). In most chapters, he identifies one or several "rhetoric[s] of" that guide the identity formation, position occupation, and literate acts that describe the chapters' foci.

Roots opens with three epigraphs. One shares a Hmong student's experience in an American school; another references the Hmong role assisting United States military efforts during the Vietnam War. The longest tells a traditional Hmong story that Duffy returns to frequently, in which the ancient Hmong lived in an independent, prosperous, literate nation in what is now China. The Hmong fled their homeland after being displaced by the Manchu dynasty, and in the course of their escape the Hmong 'book,' the metonym for the Hmong alphabet and knowledge of writing, fell into the waters of the Yellow River and was lost. Or it was eaten by horses as the Hmong slept, exhausted from their flight. Or it was eaten by the Hmong themselves, who were starving (22). This story ties loss of literacy to the losses of home, community stability, and political agency. Throughout Roots, pursuing and practicing various literacies remains tied to attempts at restoring or re-establishing those lost elements.

Duffy's first chapter, which argues that "histories of literacy are also histories of peoples," (23) starts long before the loss of the Hmong book. The chapter recounts a turbulent ancient Hmong history in China, the defeat by the Manchu dynasty, and Hmong settlement in Laos, then a French colony, in the nineteenth century. Later, members of the Hmong population in Laos were recruited to assist the CIA in espionage and military efforts against North Vietnam. As that war concluded, the Hmong were again displaced, this time to refugee camps in Thailand and then, for many, permanent resettlement in the United States.

Chapter 2 examines, as its subtitle says, "Hmong Writing Systems in China and Laos." Duffy focuses on the technical elements of literacy and the "rhetoric of writing systems" (56). The chapter covers early Hmong mnemotechnic writing systems and later alphabets created for the Hmong language by various nineteenth- and early twentieth-century Christian missionaries. The chapter highlights resonances between the Bible's book-based Christian salvation narrative and the notion of recovering home, political agency, and literacy from the lost Hmong book and acknowledges the irony of receiving a writing system for one's own language from an outside group.

Chapter 3 problematizes widely held notions of the Hmong as a long-preliterate culture, as well as the notion of preliteracy itself. Duffy explores how the "rhetoric of preliteracy" (61) has been used to marginalize the Hmong and to inaccurately simplify the history of their written culture. The chapter acknowledges that the Hmong culture that developed in Laos had little to no role for formal literacy but points out that Lao and French government policy limited Hmong formal education. Later, work with the CIA during the Vietnam War created another "literacy paradox" (77); many Hmong learned to read and write through CIA activities, but the aftermath of their involvement with the CIA was further upheaval and displacement—almost another loss of the Hmong book.

In-depth focus on Hmong literacy education in Laos in the twentieth century, largely supplied by "Lao village schools, the Hmong military, and missionary Christianity" (79), comprises Chapter 4, which expands on several issues from Chapter 2. This chapter identifies rhetorics of "Lao Schooling" (81), "Military Literacy" (93), and "Missionary Literacy" (107). Hmong students in Lao schools learned Laotian language literacy but also history and culture. Lao learning and cultural identity were privileged, Hmong identities marginalized. Other Hmong learned reading and writing as army scribes; still others learned to read and write from Bibles, prayer books, and song books brought by Christian missionaries. All of these literacies were offered to the Hmong by institutions that had their own goals—strengthening Lao cultural identity, running military bureaucracy, spreading Christian belief—but Duffy documents that Hmong men and women then also used these literacy skills to their own ends, writing such personal documents as letters to family and memoirs that tell their own stories from their own perspectives for their own purposes.

The narrative moves to the post-Vietnam War United States and the experiences of resettled Hmong people in Chapters 5 and 6. Chapter 5 looks at rhetorics of "Christian sponsorship," "public schooling" and "workplace writing" (126). The same pattern that had happened in Laos repeated itself, with institutionally taught literacies becoming tools for purposes different from or even in opposition to those institutions'. Many churches that assisted with resettlement of Hmong refugees offered a blend of English language and religious instruction; Hmong-language churches also developed. Language instruction that started with a religious emphasis did result in Christian conversion for many Hmong, but also in the re-purposing of literate practices for personal, business, artistic, and political ends. Hmong students' school experiences ranged from warm welcome to physical abuse for being different, and—as earlier generations had experienced in Laos—education focused on technical aspects of literacy and constructing an American cultural identity. Some students, though, then applied the skills they learned in school to academic and professional study of Hmong history that has been left out of many mainstream accounts. Again, in the workplace, Hmong men and women often learned highly technical forms of literacy, but work-related literacy also became a means to create new positions within the Hmong community, especially for many bilingual Hmong working as translators in various fields.

In Chapter 6, through rhetorics of "new gender relations" and "the Fair City" (153), Duffy examines the successes, struggles, and tensions of Hmong public life in Wasau. Many Hmong women Duffy interviewed had initially been discouraged from working or attending school by their male relatives, and those who were pursuing work or school outside the home were also often expected to continue fulfilling traditional feminine roles within it. With more education and professional and social success, many women then used their new skills to challenge and change "inequitable gender roles in Hmong culture" (170). Just as many Hmong women encountered resistance to their educational and professional efforts from within their families and communities, the Hmong community at large encountered resistance, resentment, and outright racism from some white residents of Wasau. This tension unfolds in a series of literate acts—letters to the local newspaper. The "anti-immigrant letters" (172) accused Hmong residents of welfare fraud, eating others' pets, and refusing to learn English, among other things. These letters also "suggested to a group of immigrant writers a particular kind of literacy" (172). Hmong Wasau residents then took up this suggested literacy, corrected these stereotypes. and extended invitations to productive community dialogue in their own letters to the editor. Again, Hmong rhetors used literacies and forms created and presented by others to carve out their own public positions and tell their own truths.

In a brief conclusion, Duffy reiterates his arguments about the rhetorical nature of literacy and its uses both to impose identities and positions on the Hmong and its re-appropriation by the Hmong to resist those impositions and express other, self-created identities and positions.

Writing from These Roots won the 2009 Conference on College Composition Outstanding Book Award, amidst other richly deserved acclaim. Duffy offers an enjoyable and educational read for both academic and general audiences interested in literacy, 20th-century social history, Hmong history, or immigration issues generally. He provides an introduction to an overlooked and misunderstood history. *Roots* is short enough and provides enough *in situ* background to incorporate in undergraduate courses in composition, literacy education, and social history. This book would work well as a supplemental text for students in twentieth-century American history courses or Vietnam War-specific courses. Its once-again-timely topical coverage makes it a good fit also for graduate courses in literacy education and for courses at various levels for pre-service and experienced teachers. The "rhetorics of" conceit would make the book or sections of it useful in graduate rhetoric seminars, from introductory survey courses to courses in rhetoric in immigrant communities, rhetoric of literacy education, or other special topics. To all readers, Duffy offers both a thorough overview of Hmong literacy history and a thoughtful invitation to reflect on how we conceptualize, teach, and interact with various literacies and diversities in our own communities.

Work Cited

Duffy, John M. *Writing from These Roots: Literacy in a Hmong-American Community*. Honolulu: U of Hawaii P, 2007. Print.

spring 2013

Affirming Students' Right to Their Own Language: Bridging Language Policies and Pedagogical Practice

Jerrie Cobb Scott, Dolores Y. Straker, and Laurie Katz, eds.
New York: Routledge; Urbana, Ill: NCTE, 2008. 418 pp.
ISBN: 978-0-8058-6349. $44.95.

Reviewed by Leah Durán
University of Texas at Austin

In *Affirming Students' Right to Their Own Language,* a wide variety of authors address the pedagogical implications of the 1974 National Council of Teachers of English resolution on students' rights to their own language (STROL). This resolution, revisited and reaffirmed more recently in 2003, calls for schools and teachers to respect and draw on students' linguistic diversity as both a right and a resource. This book, designed for pre- and in-service teachers as well as teacher educators, professional development consultants, and policy makers, does an excellent job illuminating what the editors describe as the "unfinished business" of the STROL resolution: what teachers can do in their classrooms everyday to uphold students' linguistic rights.

This volume covers research on how classroom practices can give students access to their own languages. These practices are closely described and placed in a national and international context. In Part I of this comprehensive volume, STROL are situated historically and legally in the history of United States policy and legislations. This is done chronologically by the editors and thematically through interviews with authors Joel Spring, Geneva Smitherman, Mary Carol Combs and Christina Rodríguez. These interviews are noteworthy not only for thoroughly contextualizing STROL but also for the vernacular style. Conversational and easily accessible, the interviews provide balance to a largely academic text. In the manner of Alim and Anzaldúa, these authors expand traditional definitions of academic discourse both by what they say and by how they say it.

Part II explores some of the ways that language policies and classroom practices have failed to give students access to their own language, the reasons behind resistance to the 1974 resolution, and the consequences of such resistance. Part III is the most applied of all of the sections, describing teachers' use of STROL to guide instruction in different contexts and with different populations. In Part IV, the book steps back into the workings of policy, this time in a global context. Part IV serves to contrast the permissive stance towards linguistic rights found in the U.S. with countries whose language policies explicitly acknowledge, protect, and defend linguistic diversity and linguistic minorities. It also highlights the links between the U.S. and other countries in a globalized world. This section serves to expand the readers' idea of what may be possible in U.S. classrooms, courts, and legislatures.

The book provides an important connection between the ideological commitment to giving students access to their language and the means with which to do this. This goal is well accomplished, particularly in Part III. The authors describe a variety of promising pedagogical techniques. The variety of settings (pre-K through 12) and languages (Spanish, Chinese, African-American Vernacular English, Greek Cypriot) and teachers' linguistic knowledge made this book useful for a wide range of audiences. Teacher educators in particular will find much of value here, including ideas to inform their research, advocacy, and work with pre-service teachers. A common criticism of edited books is uneven quality; this is not true of *Affirming Students' Right to Their Own Language*. The works included are uniformly excellent; all of the chapters are highly relevant, based on sound, diverse methodology. Together, they advance our understanding of how to respect students' linguistic rights and promote their academic achievement. Moreover, the book includes both a short and long view. It addresses how to support students now, as well as steps to address linguistic prejudices and values for future expansion of what counts as valuable literacy and linguistic practices.

Affirming Students' Right to Their Own Language encompasses wide territory, perhaps in an attempt to reach the many audiences identified by the editors in the introduction. The book contains multiple theoretical frameworks with which to understand student language, the core of the book. Some present STROL as a moral imperative: "the right of children to speak the language or dialect their mother loves them in," (Meyer, 54). Others, like Mari Haneda and Danling Fu, present powerful pedagogies that draw on language as a resource and an instrument for effective teaching. In their chapter on indigenous language policies and practices, Dorothy Aguilera and Margaret D. LeCompte frame language as part of Native identity and the historical struggle for greater tribal autonomy. These different theories of language are left to the reader to reconcile. For example, Rebecca Wheeler's chapter describes the usefulness of contrastive analysis (CA) as a technique for expanding students' linguistic repertoires; in contrast, David Kirkland and Austin Jackson's chapter, also on the uses of CA with African-American Language, concludes that the technique alone will not remove students' negative attitudes about the worth of their own language. While not contradictory, these two chapters in concert are at different points along a spectrum of language ideologies.

This presentation of multiple viewpoints may stem from the editors' goal of serving multiple audiences, many of whom differ in their background knowledge and beliefs about language. Several of the authors that write here about their work with pre-service teachers describe this group as primarily monolingual, middle-class and possessing internalized mainstream ideologies about the correctness of Standard English. The same generalization can be made of the general teacher population (Lippi-Green, 1996). This implies that some of the book's intended audience may resist or question the book's premise. Nor do all of the chapters *necessarily* challenge standard language ideologies; some, in isolation, might primarily serve as guides to help students acquire Standard English more effectively. This multiplicity of frameworks is both a strength and a weakness. It means that even a skeptical audience will likely find something valuable and usable, particularly in the sections that position language as an instrument for academic success. However, not every piece adheres to the stated purpose of affirming language as a right.

This book would have been even stronger had it detailed more thoroughly the extent to which hybridity and code-switching constitute valid linguistic practices in themselves (Martínez, 2009). A reader new to the field might come to understand that code-meshing and code-switching serve as a transitional phase before fluency, rather than a normal practice of multilingual speakers in plurilingual communities (Canagarajah, 2006). Manawwar Hock's chapter on multilingualism in India highlights this, but few others do explicitly. This, however, is a relatively minor criticism and does little to detract from the book's worth.

Overall, the book does an excellent job increasing our understanding of how practices and policies can better support students. Throughout, language policies and practices are considered as they relate to students as whole people. In presenting student language as both a resource and a right, it advances the goal of making schools more humane places for students who are currently marginalized. *Affirming Students' Right to Their Own Language* provides important pedagogical insight and at the same time helps envision what macro and micro policy changes will be necessary to create a more just future for multilingual and multilectal students.

Work Cited

Alim, H. Samy. "You Know My Steez: An Ethnographic and Sociolinguistic Study of Styleshifting in a Black American Speech Community." *American Speech* 89 (2004).

Anzaldúa, Gloria. *Borderlands/La Frontera: The New Mestiza*. San Francisco: Aunt Lute Books, 1999.

Canagarajah, Suresh. "The Place of World Englishes in Composition: Pluralization Continued." *College Composition and Communication* 57:4 (2006): 586–619.

Lippi-Green, Rosina. *English with an Accent: Language, Ideology, and Discrimination in the United States*. London: Routledge, 1997.

Martínez, Ramon Antonio. "Spanglish as Literacy Tool: Toward an Understanding of the Potential Role of Spanish-English Code-Switching in the Development of Academic Literacy." *Research in the Teaching of English* 45:2 (2010): 124-49.

Writing in Rhythm: Spoken Word Poetry in Urban Classrooms

Maisha T. Fisher

NY, NY: Teachers College Press, 2007. 128 pp.
ISBN: 080774770X. $22.95

Youth Poets: Empowering Literacies In and Out of Schools

Korina M. Jocson

NY, NY: Peter Lang Publishing, 2008. 214 pp.
ISBN: 0820481963. $35.95

Reviewed by Lance Langdon
University of California, Irvine

Fisher and Jocson both make the case that those involved in public rhetoric and community-based literacy ought to pay more attention to poetry, particularly that created by urban youth. By tracing the roots of contemporary spoken-word poetry to hip-hop, blues, and the Black Arts movement, both studies suggest that poetry has long bridged out-of-school and school-based literacies. For these authors, poetry is a rhetoric that at once celebrates the vernacular and builds coalitions amongst disenfranchised groups.

In *Writing in Rhythm: Spoken Word Poets in Urban Classrooms*, Maisha Fisher documents the year she shadowed Joseph Ubiles, a high school teacher and coalition builder in the Bronx. Fisher watches, and occasionally jumps in, as Ubiles leads a spoken-word class called Power Writers. Fisher's ethnography is a pleasure to read, with a brisk and vivid delivery of the poetry workshops and thick description of the cultural contexts that inform them. Her authority is often on display, as when she frames her observations with educational theories, such as Freire's participatory classroom, and history. But she wears that learning lightly and uses it to illuminate the day-to-day of the workshops.

The book's title might suggest that its message applies only to schools, but Fisher's previous works have addressed the knowledge and practices of poets working open mics at neighborhood institutions, particularly Black-owned bookstores in Northern California. One of her research questions probes the degree to which the literacies that operate in these spaces intersect with those in the titular urban "classrooms." Thus, *Writing in Rhythm* takes public ground not just when Joe Ubiles acquaints his students with the Nuyorican Poetry Café, the Cloisters, the Upper West Side, the Brooklyn Botanical Gardens, or the Apollo Theater. It also makes the case that Joe's role as a literacy educator places him in the tradition of community memory-keepers, people like the book and magazine vendors of Greenwich Village, respected as "old heads" for the wisdom they have earned through their own experience and through witnessing the experiences of their fellows (83).

It is in this tradition of witnessing that Fisher places herself as she passes on Joe's and the students' idiolect. She writes, "the role of a worthy witness is keeping the naming actions of the community intact" (17). Chapter 4, "We Speak in all Tongues: The Politics of Bronxonics" is thus particularly useful as a reminder of the power of "non-standard" English to name the communities in which we live. Bronxonics, we learn, includes elements of both African-American Vernacular English and Puerto Rican- and Dominican-inflected Spanish. Echoing Joe, Fisher argues that this linguistic "gumbo" contains not just a lovely "magic" of rhythm and tone, but also the "money" that young people need to make their way through the day (45). Fisher reminds readers that the "civic" space of civic engagement does not always accept academic language as currency, and stresses "how important it was not to leave our students 'naked' when putting them out into the world," by stripping them of their home language (44). Accordingly, Joe teaches not academese or the vernacular, but both. As one of his students puts it, "[Joe]'s saying adapt to your environment. Let people know you are street smart and book smart" (44).

Maisha's and Joe's decision to honor these poets as "[t]rustworthy witnesses to love, heartache, poverty, violence, and struggles for understanding" pays off in the "blues" poems she brings forth in Chapter 6, which comment on these experiences with clarity and force (69). Fisher begins by deftly summarizing scholarly debates over the degree to which rap develops or departs from the blues tradition, and then argues that spoken word poetry has a "blues epistemology," and thus that blues and rap are "the roots" of contemporary poetry (68). In their poems, the Power Writers as often choose "standard English" as "the idiolect of the street" to testify regarding cycles of young motherhood, drug addiction, intra-group racism, and the failures of state agencies charged with health and education (79). Throughout, Maisha sheds light on the students' poems by illuminating their cultural contexts, from Colombian cumbia to the use of "Spanish" as a local term for Dominicans or Puerto Ricans. One young writer states that "[t]he ghetto is indescribable to those who have never lived there," but with her help and Fisher's, readers of this volume develop a sense of the inner-city as a dispiriting "mental place" (75).

Fisher does not hide the difficulties for Power Writers in engaging with students' personal experience so searchingly, as when she narrates a class session in which students mock-cry and wail so as to avoid "carrying the weight" of a poet's sadness over her abandonment by her father. But Fisher also acknowledges that work's potential to promote a literacy that reaches beyond the classroom, for she argues convincingly that spoken-word poetry can move poets and listeners alike to upend the "confusing vernacular" of dominant narratives that speak of the failures and deficits of urban youth (31). Ubiles's students learn that poetry can be, as June Jordan says, a "medium for telling the truth" *(Blueprint* 36). And Fisher argues that such truth can begin to effect urgently needed social change. Indeed, perhaps the book's broadest message is that we all suffer, albeit unequally, from what Joe calls the "higher mathematics of America"—our society's disproportionate incarceration of urban youth, our stifling of their talent, and our ignorance of their knowledge (99).

Chapter 7 wraps up the monograph on a more hopeful note, extrapolating from the Power Writers program to make suggestions for other language arts programs within and beyond K-12 public schools. One such suggestion is that educators "create a curriculum for and with students that confronts issues that are relevant" to them (93). In Ubiles's case that curriculum is poetry, and one of his students marks out the difference between Power Writers and the typical class quote simply: "Poetry is about us. In English class the curriculum is about them. The school's work" (ibid). Creating a student-driven curriculum is a difficult task, but Fisher argues that it is essential if educators are to stop using school language as a tool to "create distance between people and reify status and power" (98). Instead, Fisher suggests that students and teachers must make connections with one another and listen and respond to each other's stories in a process Joe calls "read and feed." Actions as simple as "[h]olding student work up for attention, even when it still needs improvement," Fisher argues, are steps that teachers as healers can take toward creating a more respectful society (92). How such affirmation can be squared with the gatekeeping function of writing programs, which are often charged with sorting students into "proficient" and "remedial" categories so as to more efficiently build their skills, is an open question. Reading this text in a graduate course in rhet-comp or teacher education would be useful in provoking literacy educators to face up to the costs of the gatekeeping and policing functions we serve when we neglect nonstandard English.

If there is one difficulty that Fisher glosses over, it is the challenge of translating the Power Writers' practices into other environments. As an experienced public school educator, Fisher must know that the individualized attention Joe gives to his students in this small elective course is more difficult to deliver in a standard thirty-plus student class. Fisher acknowledges that it is not enough to suggest that a given school could be saved if there were "10 Joes" or "50 Joes," but it is sometimes difficult to imagine how Joe's knowledge and practices could transfer to other settings. For instance, one wonders how literacy educators that do not share their students' backgrounds can be as responsive as this "old head" is to writers' particular learning blocks or their resistance.

Korina Jocson's *Youth Poets: Empowering Literacies In and Out of Schools* would perhaps answer that last question by suggesting that universities make better use of the college students from underrepresented communities who are already in their midst. For Jocson, too, describes poetry workshops that take place in high school classrooms, but these workshops involve undergraduates from U.C. Berkeley's "Poetry for the People" (P4P) program as poets and teachers.

In her introduction, Jocson writes, "Dozens of poetry programs and organizations across the country have adopted P4P's blueprint" (8). Perhaps those imitators made use of P4P founder June Jordan's 1995 volume, *Poetry for the People, a Revolutionary Blueprint*. Though Jocson's study can be understood on its own terms, Jordan's earlier text more dramatically illuminates the larger shape and purpose of P4P, and readers interested in bringing poetry to the people in their own communities will find the earlier text more inspiring. At once irreverent and earnest, urgent and classic, the *Blueprint* opens with Jordan's manifesto on a people's poetry and follows with a range of useful P4P artifacts: Jordan's syllabi; her tips for effective teaching, for "staging a revolutionary reading," and for "getting the word out" through publicity; essays by poet-scholars like Adrienne Rich; poems written by the (now famous) alumni of P4P; and even several lists (now slightly outdated) of American multicultural poetry.

Jordan died in 2002, but P4P continues. The program's longevity is testament not just to Jordan's vision, but to the infrastructure she built: a "fully accredited, three-part series composed of three African American Studies upper division courses" (Jocson 8). In a university system that too often treats students as receptacles, P4P's educational model is indeed revolutionary; undergrads who stick with P4P through the second and third courses become Student-Teacher-Poets (STPs), first leading their college peers during poetry workshops, and later teaching poetry in local high schools, prisons, and churches.

Korina Jocson was herself a STP, and both her earlier articles and this study grow out of that work. Here, Jocson addresses the youths' poetry as "process, product, and practice" by gathering a rich set of data: field notes; interviews with students, teachers, and STPs; secondary students' poetry notebooks and anthologies; and students' academic records (57). Using these, the study makes good on its claim to "make sense of poetry as a cultural form present in urban youth culture" and to highlight poetry's promise for "culturally relevant teaching in various learning settings" (27). Much like Fisher, Jocson argues that poetry "legitimizes students' sense of knowing" and "provide[s] students the opportunity to critically examine the sociocultural world in which they live" (30). And it does so in a form that, according to June Jordan, demands "the utmost precision in the use of language, hence, density and intensity of expression" (36).

It must be said that the book, which clocks in at about two hundred pages, takes its time laying out its theory and methodology in the early chapters. Jocson pulls from a wide and impressive array of literacy scholars including Vygotsky, Scribner and Cole, Emig, Bakhtin, and Brian Street. But as in much academic work, this diverse literature can become a liability to a reader wishing to tie the book together under what Elenore Long might call a "guiding metaphor." That is, Jocson accurately applies others' theories of literacy to P4P but is not interested in providing a new theory through which to view literacy. It is sometimes unclear which of the many theoretical traditions she draws from best explains P4P's work at Bellevue High. The result is that Chapter 2: Critical Multiculturalism and Ethnography, which clearly lays out how the author's background as a child of immigrants and a graduate of an urban public school prepares her for this work, is less clear about the ways in which "critical multiculturalism" shapes that work or how it might shape the work of others investigating community-based literacy.

Readers looking for a quicker read might thus be forgiven for jumping into the thick of things in Chapter 3, which introduces the study's primary site—Bellevue High. The school tells a depressingly familiar story: 80-90% of its White and Asian graduates are eligible for admission to California's state colleges based on their high-school coursework, but only about half of its Latino and Black graduates can say the same. This diverse school, Jocson argues, "implicitly reWsegregates its students on the basis of race, class, and ability" (63). P4P intervenes in the education of students of color at Bellevue by bringing college poets to their classrooms. Three times a week for six weeks, they join in workshops to pen poems whose topics include racial profiling, democracy and love. Each six-week session culminates with a public reading.

Jocson does not shy away from documenting the occasional missed connections between undergraduates and high school students, but what appears most clearly is the undergraduates' success. Jocson suggests that P4P poets, many of whom identify as underrepresented minorities and some of whom attended high schools similar to Bellevue, are well-equipped to help the younger students grow as writers and to make the college connection. "[E]thnic and cultural composition matter," Jocson argues, as students "begin to build social relationships" that inform their literacies (104). She adds that the STPs' "shared knowledge about youth popular culture" and "youthful demeanor" enables them to reach the younger students in ways their teachers find difficult (174).

The book's tour de force is Chapter 6, in which Jocson focuses on the richly literate lives of the seven youths she tracks. She finds them writing on buses, reading magazines, taking notes on underground artists, writing poems to family members and peers, performing at poetry slams (one student advances to regional competition), and even interning at a youth-run radio station. These multiple forms of literacy suggest that the school is only one of many sponsors in a city-wide literacy ecology not unlike the one Goldblatt finds in the Philadelphia of *Because We Live Here*.

Maisha Fisher's *Writing in Rhythm* is the more gripping text. It sustains its focus on the Power Writers' eloquent poetry. And its transcripts of classroom conversations vividly present how a skilled teacher "feeds" burgeoning poets and cultivates young people's ability to do the same. However, for the reader looking for guidance in stepping back and considering how such teacherly virtues might be applied in a different context, Jocson's book has the edge. For Jocson's final chapter offers explicit suggestions to those who would adapt P4P's methods—and not all turn on poetry in the secondary classroom. For example, community literacy practitioners will appreciate Jocson's suggestion that we "keep up to date with local youth groups and literary arts organizations," their events and publications (177). And readers of this study (and Jordan's *Blueprint*) will come away with a logistical understanding of how Berkeley's partnerships develop "extracurricular" literacy practices like spoken-word poetry. This is not to say that P4P's strategies can be easily replicated. It takes time to create poetry performances that gather larger audiences, and it takes money to sponsor competitions that do the same (many of these students submitted their work for the $1,000 June Jordan poetry prize). But the thought-provoking poetry that Jocson showcases throughout her monograph makes a strong case that such efforts pay off.

Indeed, it is hard to put down either of these volumes without the abiding conviction that poetry can once again play a central role in public rhetoric. As June Jordan writes, "Good poems can interdict a suicide, rescue a love affair, and build a revolution in which speaking and listening to somebody becomes the first and last purpose of every social encounter" (3). Together, these volumes allow readers to listen to the too often neglected voices of urban youth, delivering both the weight of their insights and the force of their critique.

The Hard Work of Imagining: The Inaugural Summit of the National Consortium of Writing Across Communities
Albuquerque, NM. July 12-15, 2012

Reviewed by Brian Hendrickson
University of New Mexico

On July 12-15, 2012, in advance of the Council of Writing Program Administrators 2012 Conference in Albuquerque, New Mexico, the University of New Mexico hosted the inaugural Summit of the National Consortium of Writing Across Communities (NCWAC) in nearby Santa Fe. In attendance were twenty-four established and emerging scholars and graduate students working in (and across) fields such as community literacy, writing program administration, writing across the curriculum, and second-language writing. Of NCWAC's twenty-seven sponsoring institutions, represented at the summit in addition to the host university were Arizona State University, University of Arkansas, Bridgewater State University, University of California Santa Barbara, Colorado State University, Georgia Institute of Technology, University of Oklahoma, St. John's University, Salt Lake Community College, Temple University, Texas A&M University-Commerce, and University of Utah. The purpose of the summit, like that of the consortium itself, was to bring these scholars and their respective disciplines into conversation, with a recognition that the next generation of public intellectuals must, according to Ellen Cushman, "combine their research, teaching, and service efforts in order to address social issues important to community members in under-served neighborhoods" (329).

Established at the historic Mary Mac's Tea Room in Atlanta, Georgia, during the 2011 Conference on College Composition and Communication, NCWAC arose out of a constellation of conversations led by scholars such as Linda Adler-Kassner, John Duffy, Linda Flower, Keith Gilyard, Eli Goldblatt, Juan Guerra, Michelle Hall Kells, Elenore Long, Steve Parks, Jacqueline Jones Royster, and John Trimbur, to name a few; each scholar's work, distributed along the spectrum of literacy advocacy and instruction, to coordinates—and the connections between them—overlooked or undervalued by traditional approaches to academic writing instruction. In the spirit of sustaining those conversations, NCWAC derived its name from Juan Guerra and Michelle Hall Kells' argument for a cultural ecology approach to cultivating what Guerra terms *transcultural citizenship*: "adaptive strategies that help individuals move across cultural boundaries by negotiating new and different contexts and communicative conventions" (296-99). This approach manifested in 2005 in the University of New Mexico's Writing Across Communities Initiative, which holds that "communicative competence depends upon complex strategies of shuttling between ideas and audiences, a challenging, culturally-dependent process" (Kells 96). Writing Across Communities therefore complements the notion of a writing beyond the curriculum model of writing program administration forwarded by Steve Parks and Eli Goldblatt, in which students, instructors and administrators "think through and across and outside disciplines" (Parks and Goldblatt 589).

Writing Across Communities adds to this ongoing conversation an important contextual and ethical qualifier by framing literacy initiatives within a cultural ecology model, thereby "resist[ing] a culture-blind mode of document production and seek[ing] to guide students to critically respond to the cultural and symbolic systems within diverse contexts" (Kells 98). This mission requires not only that writing instruction across the curriculum must more explicitly "enhanc[e] opportunities to build identification with the cultures of the academy" but also "cultivate appreciation across the university for the cultures and epistemologies our students bring with them" (Kells 96). Writing Across Communities, then, makes an important contribution to the ongoing conversation calling for a radical re-envisioning of the academic mission in light of recent developments in fields invested in literacy advocacy and instruction. However, advocates for this re-envisioning, in performing public intellectual work in service to the most vulnerable communities within their spheres of influence, are likely to render themselves vulnerable to those forces in the academy invested in maintaining conventional modes of disciplinary knowledge-making and professionalization—modes that still hold sway over programmatic missions and tenure review boards inclined to apply to public intellectual work the pejorative *service*. Furthermore, this new imperative requires a breadth of interdisciplinary knowledge and administrative responsibility far beyond the pale of any one individual's capabilities, so scholars committed to this work would need to be able to plug into some kind of network designed for sharing knowledge and resources across institutions.

These shared concerns provided the exigence for the inaugural NCWAC Summit, an intimate gathering of stakeholders charged with imagining how a national consortium might support emerging public intellectuals in pursuing their scholarly agendas. The three-day program was structured so that Thursday, July 12, and Friday, July 13, each began with attendees delivering position statements informing, qualifying, and problematizing the formation and implementation of a National Consortium of Writing Across Communities. Among those statements were calls for clarifying disciplinary foci and programmatic and organizational missions, increasing mentorship opportunities for graduate students of color, responding to the needs of second-language writers across the disciplines, and cultivating multimodal literacies on campus and in the community. Although these statements tended to reinforce the need for supporting graduate students and emerging scholars doing public intellectual work, the range of concerns represented even in the above summary list hints at some of the issues to emerge during the working group sessions following the delivery of position statements on Thursday and Friday.

The five working groups were charged with brainstorming an organizational mission/vision statement, professional/intellectual statement, organizational structure, terms of membership, and web presence. After the working group sessions on Thursday and Friday, the summit reconvened to share their findings, with each working group often reporting more questions than answers. One question that resonated throughout the working groups related to what the consortium should call itself given that any label it adopted would carry its own discipline-specific history and connotations likely to exclude those who would not identify with a particular disciplinary tradition. A related question asked how the consortium might constitute itself so as to remain a loose, inclusive collective while retaining some unifying sense of mission. Both questions evidenced the enduring influence of the academy's silo effect even on scholars who perceived their work as transgressing disciplinary boundaries as traditionally conceived.

What became increasingly obvious over the course of Thursday and Friday was a difference in perception—between established scholars on the one hand, and on the other, graduate students and emerging scholars—regarding the two above questions, with the former perceiving them as impediments calling into question the efficacy of a National Consortium of Writing Across Communities, and the latter interpreting the questions either as a generative heuristic or irrelevant barrier in establishing a consortium aimed at addressing the common concerns reflected in attendees' position statements. In order to address this aporia of perspective, then, Saturday's meeting began with a freewrite asking each attendee to respond anonymously in writing to the following prompt: "What is it that we share in common, but doesn't necessarily make us the same, that we can get from this consortium but can't get anywhere else?" After approximately ten minutes of writing, the freewrites were collected, shuffled, and redistributed to be read aloud to the group. Thereafter the floor was open to response under one condition: that speakers frame their remarks in terms of what they heard rather than their own opinions on the matter.

Despite the differences in perspective that had become increasingly apparent over the course of the summit, emerging from the conversation that followed was a recognition of the importance of valuing community, both as an object of scholarship as well as a network of scholars themselves. Both established and emerging scholars repeatedly remarked on the invigorating nature of the summit in terms of the intimacy of the small-group setting as well as the interdisciplinary exchange of ideas. For the graduate students, the conversation was instructive as to the complexities of collaborating across disciplines even in a group that shares a common set of values and goals, but it also provided important opportunities for them to meet and receive advice from scholars they admired.

Ultimately it was decided that the conversation would have to be continued at the 2013 Conference on College Composition and Communication in Las Vegas, Nevada, with Michelle Cox volunteering to host a lunch, and Todd Ruecker a hike.

But the conversation didn't end there. Throughout Saturday afternoon and into Sunday, small groups continued to meet and reflect on the summit, both its problems and potentialities. And at dinner that evening just north of Santa Fe, in the small town of Chimayó, in a restaurant not far from the miraculous Santuario de Nuestro Señor de Esquipulas, a raucous group of graduate students and emerging scholars joked about changing the name from the contested NCWAC to WI-B-WAC (Writing In, Beyond, With and Across Communities). Whatever it is called, the joke seemed to suggest, the need remains for the establishment of a supportive community of literacy-scholars-as-public-intellectuals—one that can be accessed by and efficacious for our most vulnerable colleagues, such as prospective and current graduate students, contingent faculty, and those going up for tenure.

Works Cited

Cushman, Ellen. "The Public Intellectual, Service Learning, and Activist Research." *College English* 61.3 (1999): 328-36.

Guerra, Juan C. "Writing for Transcultural Citizenship: A Cultural Ecology Model." *Language Arts* 85.4 (2008): 296-304.

Kells, Michelle Hall. "Writing Across Communities: Deliberation and the Discursive Possibilities of WAC." *Reflections* 6.1 (2007): 87-108.

Parks, Steve, and Eli Goldblatt. "Writing beyond the Curriculum: Fostering New Collaborations in Literacy." *College English* 62:5 (2000): 584-606.

New Releases . . .

A Rhetoric for Writing Program Administrators
Edited by Rita Malenczyk. 471 pages. $40 (paperback); $80 (cloth); $25 (digital)

Class Politics: The Movement for the Students' Right to Their Own Language (2e)
Stephen Parks. 363 pages. $32 (paperback); $65 (cloth); $20 (digital)

Po H# on Dope to Ph.D.: How Education Saved My Life
Elaine Richardson. 263 pages. $22.95 (paperback); $20 (digital). New Community Press

Mics, Cameras, Symbolic Action: Audio-Visual Rhetoric for Writing Teachers
Bump Halbritter. 275 pages. $32 (paperback); $65 (cloth); $20 (digital)

The WPA Outcomes Statement—A Decade Later
Edited by Nicholas N. Behm, Gregory R. Glau, Deborah H. Holdstein, Duane Roen, and Edward M. White. 344 pages. $32 (paperback); $65 (cloth); $20 (digital).

Writing Program Administration at Small Liberal Arts Colleges
Jill M. Gladstein and Dara Rossman Regaignon. 290 pages. $32 (paperback); $60 (cloth); $20 (digital)

Read more about forthcoming releases for the iPad and tablet computers, events celebrating our tenth year as a scholarly publisher, and more at

www.parlorpress.com

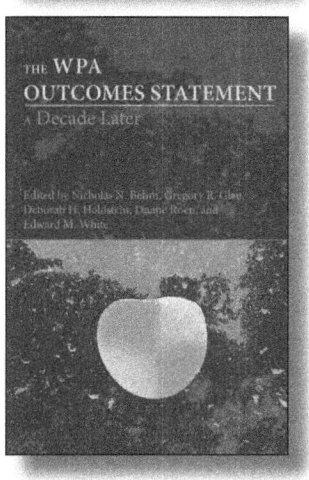

DEPAUL UNIVERSITY
Chicago, IL

DEPARTMENT OF
WRITING, RHETORIC, & DISCOURSE

Master of Arts Degrees in
NEW MEDIA STUDIES
WRITING, RHETORIC, & DISCOURSE
with concentrations in
PROFESSIONAL & TECHNICAL WRITING
TEACHING WRITING & LANGUAGE

Graduate certificate in TESOL
Combined BA/MA in Writing, Rhetoric, & Discourse

GRADUATE FACULTY
Matthew Abraham
Julie Bokser
Darsie Bowden
Antonio Ceraso
Rene De los Santos
Lisa Dush
Jason Kalin
Sarah Read
Christine Tardy
Peter Vandenberg

WRD.DEPAUL.EDU

www.ingramcontent.com/pod-product-compliance
Lightning Source LLC
Chambersburg PA
CBHW031350160426
43196CB00007B/799